Achieving Your
BEST

Self

Fast Track Your Efforts To Achieving Your Highest Goals

Dr David Noel Barton

Lone Tree
Publishers
Dunedin, New Zealand

David Barton Training
PO Box 8009
Gardens, Dunedin, 9041
Otago, New Zealand
www.davidbartontraining.com
Email: davidbarton@davidbartontraining.com

Disclaimer

Although the author has made every effort to ensure that the information in this book was correct at press time, the author does not assume and hereby disclaim any liability to any party for any loss, damage, or disruption caused by errors or omissions, whether such errors or omissions result from negligence, accident, or any other cause. While we try to keep the information up-to-date and correct, there are no representations or warranties, expressed or implied, about the completeness, accuracy, reliability, suitability or availability with respect to the information, products, services, or related graphics contained in this program for any purpose. Any use of this information is at your own risk.

Ordering Information

Special discounts are available on quantity purchases by corporations, associations, and others. For details, contact the publisher at the address above.

ISBN: 978-0-473-37193-7

Editing/Proofreading by Kate Morrison.

ACKNOWLEDGMENTS

This book is dedicated to my Lord and Saviour Jesus Christ, my loving wife Ruan and our three beautiful daughters Rebekah, Abigail and Hannah and my mother Pearl, who have always supported me in achieving my best self. Without all of you none of this would be possible.

CONTENTS

CHAPTER 1

Time is Not On Your Side

"My favourite things in life don't cost any money. It's really clear that the most precious resource we all have is time."

Steve Jobs

It is day one and the clock has started ticking. You have arrived in the delivery room. Everyone is so delighted to see you – they have been waiting here for quite some time – not just in the delivery room, but here on planet Earth you now will also call your home. For you though, this is day one, the first day of the rest of your life. From this day forth your time will be a diminishing resource, and you are now on the same *time* treadmill as everyone else. Your world is new, strange and filled with novelty, and at this very moment you have absolutely no idea what you are going to do with your life.

Several years have passed, and you now have some valuable life experience under your belt. Unlike that first day when you first appeared you have grown significantly. As you are reading this book, I expect you have reached the point in life where you are beginning to question your purpose for being here. If you are like me, you will want to live the best life you can, and achieve the most you are able to achieve with what time you have been given.

Possibly you might want to know if there are any secrets to using your time more efficiently – for instance, are there ways of optimising your efforts to achieve your dreams faster and enjoy them while you still can. Let's face it, who doesn't want to work less, but still have enough money to travel, own a house or two, be debt free early in life, and buy a new car every few years or so. Most of us would relish the opportunity to spend quality time each day with the people we love, without constant worry of how we going to pay the bills and keep our heads above the many responsibilities we have to contend with.

By studying and observing successful people, I have discovered that they have learned to lead more productive lives. At some level they appear to have learned or stumbled upon, the keys to success.

These keys to success have been peddled as secrets by some, but are really not secrets at all. These 'secrets' are commonly known to the masses, but most people simply do not follow them. Author of *The Slight Edge: Secret to a Successful Life,* Jeff Olson, said, "Successful people do what unsuccessful people are not willing to do."[61] The fact is, successful people spend their time in distinctly different ways, compared to less successful people.

Author, Jim Rohm, said, "an obvious, yet often overlooked truth is that rich people have 24 hours a day and poor people have 24 hours a day. The difference between the rich and the poor is the management of that time. Successful people often work harder and longer than most, but they almost always work smarter."[67]

Successful people focus less on the trivial, and more on the monumental. They spend less time on the small, inconsequential tasks and issues, and more time on their most important goals and priorities.

Prioritizing time is one of the *Big Ideas* of this book. Successful people have achieved success largely because they have discovered their focal point, and then fixated all their energy onto that one point. Increasing productivity is not just about learning to do things faster, but more importantly, it is about learning to do the right things faster.

Time: The Great Equalizer

Time is the great equalizer of us all. Time does not discriminate by favouring the strong, successful or wealthy. You can't buy more time, and it makes no difference if you are born into the Royal family, or the slums of Calcutta. Time is neither your friend, nor your enemy. Time gives everyone the same measure each day: 24 hours, 1440 minutes or 84,400 seconds. Time is finite, you cannot manufacture it. You can make more money, but you cannot make more time. Time is the most valuable thing you can give to another person, because it is something you can never get back again.

Time is unmanageable, thus the term *Time Management* is an oxymoron. But, even though you cannot manage time itself, you can manage what activities you do in the time you have been given. You cannot control time, but you can control yourself, and this is what it means to have self-control. You have the power to decide what you will do to fill your time.

Successful people fill their time differently to the way unsuccessful people fill theirs, and in this book I will reveal to you how you can change the way you fill your time. I believe every person should have a sense of urgency to learn as much as they can about managing their short visit in our world. Your time could elapse before you can blink an eye. James says, "What is your life? You are a mist that appears for a little while and then vanishes." (James 4:14: NIV). The length of this mist will vary from person to person, but irrespective of its length, we should all be doing our best to maximise each moment we have and live the best life we can.

How much time do you really have? That is the million dollar question. If you could find out the answer right now, would that change the way you currently spend your time, and live your life? Would knowledge of your end date cause you to change the plans you set for today? According to a report released by the Population Division of the United Nations Department of Economic and Social Affairs (UN DESA)(July 2014), life expectancy is far better for people living in developed countries than for those living in developing countries. If you live in Japan you're in luck, as people there typically live to the ripe old age of 83.7 years. Other countries with an age expectancy over 80 include; Hong Kong (83.5), Switzerland (82.7), and New Zealand (81.6). Usually females live longer than males, but the difference is marginal. Contrast this to some of the least fortunate places to live, where countries have an age expectancy lower than 50 years, for instance; Central African Republic (45.9), Lesotho (46.02) and Sierra Leone (46.26).

So depending on where you live, you might live into your 80's. That is a respectable amount of time to live, in anyone's books. But, there are no guarantees. You could be in a freak accident tomorrow. You might have an incurable medical problem, or physical defect. Of course, living in a first world country does not guarantee you a long life. For many people, their time on earth is cut short by all sorts of eventualities no one could have seen coming. For example, author Eugene O'Kelly chronicles the last days of his life in his moving book "Chasing Daylight: How My Forthcoming Death Transformed my Life."[60]

At age 53, O'Kelly was diagnosed with late-stage brain cancer, and given just 3 to 6 months to live. The day before his diagnosis he was in full swing of his career; he was Chairman and CEO of KPMG, one of the largest accounting firms in the U.S. O'Kelly had a loving family and close friends. He had plans for the future, a schedule booked out months in advance, and many things he still wanted to do with his life. Then in May 2005, he was abruptly yanked out of the world he once knew, and thrown into one he was scarcely prepared for. *Chasing Daylight* is an account of the last days he had with his loved ones, his process of gaining deeper understanding of his condition, and the unwinding and dissolution of the relationships he once had. O'Kelly's story serves to remind us to make the most of our opportunities while we still can, because tomorrow is not guaranteed to any of us, irrespective of what country we are living in.

Bestselling author, Og Mandino, whose books sold well over 50 million copies worldwide, once said, "Tomorrow is only found in the calendar of fools." He believed that you should live each day as if it were your last. Mandino said, "Beginning today, treat everyone you meet as if they were going to be dead by midnight. Extend to them all the care, kindness and understanding you can muster, and do it with no thought of any reward. Your life will never be the same again." These words have a tone of finality and do not reflect a blasé, indifferent attitude to people and time. What a different world we would live in, if everyone was to treat others with the respect and kindness typically shown to someone who was not going to be around tomorrow.

Quality Versus Quantity

Quantity of time is very different to quality of time. There are many people who have lived lives with a richness of experience so great that their one life could easily equate to the combined experiences of several others who have done little or nothing of note. When I refer to quality, I mean living your life without repetition. I mean not spending each day doing the same things, over and over again, repeating the same experience you had countless times before. It reminds me of the movie *Groundhog Day* (1993) staring Bill Murray, a weather man, and co-starring Andy MacDowell, who played the producer of the weather reports. [1]

Murray travels to a town to report on an annual festival in which a Groundhog foretells the arrival of an early spring, a festival which he reported many times before, and one which he is reluctant to report any longer. However, this time he finds himself reliving the same day over and over again. Every morning his life resets to the

---

[1] If you want to watch another excellent movie with a similar theme see Tom Cruise in Edge of Tomorrow (2014)

same day, which only he knows is happening. He tries in vain to convince MacDowell that he has lived the same day many times before. He can predict events with such perfect accuracy, which only someone who had been there before would know. But convincing others of his *life on repeat* predicament is all but impossible, and on the off chance that one day he is making progress, night comes and the next day arrives. Everything and everyone is reset, and he has to try and convince them all over again.

Everyone is oblivious that he has experienced the same day before. Murray, on the other hand, is fully cognisant of the fact, and this eventually takes its toll on him. Once Murray accepts his fate, he begins to change his attitude. He starts acquiring new skills, and performs hundreds of acts of kindness. By the end of the movie, Murray has transformed himself from a self-centered jerk, to a talented, helpful and generous man. It is a wonderful movie, and it is not far from the truth of how many people live their lives. The fact is, much of life is lived on repeat. We constantly replay our lives, like a DJ replaying the same song over, and over again. Unlike Murray, we don't get to reset today and improve tomorrow, and once our day is gone, it is gone forever. We do have an advantage over Murray; we don't have to live our lives on repeat, unless we choose to. Each day we can start anew, and decide to live it better than the day before.

What People Say Who Have Run Out Of Time

In her book *Top 5 regrets of the dying*[83], Bronnie Ware, recorded her patients dying epiphanies. Ware is an Australian nurse who spent several years working in palliative care, and wrote a blog called *Inspiration and Chai*. Her blog became the source of her book. Ware said, "When questioned about any regrets they had or anything they would do differently…common themes surfaced again and again."

The Top 5 Themes

1. **I wish I'd had the courage to live a life true to myself, not the life others expected of me.** "This was the most common regret of all. When people realise that their life is almost over and look back clearly on it, it is easy to see how many dreams have gone unfulfilled. Most people had not honoured even a half of their dreams and had to die knowing that it was due to choices they had made, or not made. Health brings a freedom very few realise, until they no longer have it."

2. **I wish I hadn't worked so hard.** "This came from every male patient that I nursed. They missed their children's youth and their partner's companionship. Women also spoke of this regret, but as most were from an older generation, many of the female patients had not been breadwinners. All of the men I nursed deeply regretted spending so much of their lives on the treadmill of a work existence."

3. **I wish I'd had the courage to express my feelings.** "Many people suppressed their feelings in order to keep peace with others. As a result, they settled for a mediocre existence and never became who they were truly capable of becoming. Many developed illnesses relating to the bitterness and resentment they carried as a result."

4. **I wish I had stayed in touch with my friends.** "Often they would not truly realise the full benefits of old friends until their dying weeks and it was not always possible to track them down. Many had become so caught up in their own lives that they had let golden friendships slip by over the years. There were many deep regrets about not giving friendships the time and effort that they deserved. Everyone misses their friends when they are dying."

5. **I wish that I had let myself be happier.** This is a surprisingly common one. Many did not realise until the end that happiness is a choice. They had stayed stuck in old patterns and habits.

The so-called 'comfort' of familiarity overflowed into their emotions, as well as their physical lives. Fear of change had them pretending to others, and to their selves, that they were content, when deep within, they longed to laugh properly and have silliness in their life again.

If we take a closer look at what these people said, and what they would do more of, we don't find them mentioning spending more time at the office. A common theme to their regrets was working less, rather than more.

The American Time Use Survey collects information about what people do during the day and how much time they spend on these activities. This survey found people aged between 25 to 54, living with children under 18, spend on average 8.9 hours working, 7.7 hours sleeping, 2.5 hours doing leisurely activities, and 1.2 hours caring for others.[76]

This means they spent 54% of their waking hours working, and only 15% of their waking hours doing the things they enjoyed. It is not surprising that people who were close to dying have said they would have spent less time at work, as work had consumed so much of their lives. All you have in the end is your memories, and if your memories are dominated by work, then you will feel robbed of having lived a full life if your work was meaningless and unenjoyably. In a recent report produced by The Conference Board, a New York-based non-profit research group, 52.3% of Americans reported feeling unhappy at work.[8] Life is too short to spend it doing work you don't enjoy, so if you don't want to live a life of regret make a change now before it's too late.

Ware's interviews also found people on their deathbeds said they would have wanted to live a life with more meaning and purpose. I will discuss this topic further in another chapter, but I believe this is one of the greatest yearnings people have. I believe people have a strong desire to live a life of purpose; a life which has meaning, and a life which makes them jump out of bed in the morning. People want to live to their full potential. What rule in the universe says that you should not, cannot, or are not allowed to find happiness in your work and life? As far as I know, no such rule exists.

How Can This Book Help You?

I have written this book to help you peer under the hood of your life, and look into the recesses of your mind and spirit. My hope is that through reading this book, you will discover more of what it is you want to get out of life. I hope you will gain greater clarity, and awareness of your richest dreams and highest goals. I hope you will learn how to formulate your goals, establish your focus and set your direction.

You can apply the information from this book to your existing job or career, or to your personal life, or even forge a new path altogether. Irrespective of where you find yourself right now, you can attain greater success in your life, no matter what your endeavour is.

You are the captain of your own ship, and it is up to you to set the course, raise the sails and lift the anchor. You can decide to stay in the comfort of the harbour, or sail out into the open sea. You can be Columbus and sail into uncharted territory, discovering new lands and meeting new people, or you can look on from the sea shore as the ship sails away. Your destiny is up to you; it's in your hands. You can choose to set your own goals, or allow someone else to set them for you. In the end it is all up to you.

So what will you do with your time? I opened this chapter with these thoughts, and I will end it with the same. My hope is that you will put your time to good use, and live a life worth living, a life you will be proud to call your own.

KEY POINTS TO REMEMBER

- Achieving your best self is directly proportional to the way you spend your time.

- Time is a diminishing resource for all of us. From the time we are born, the hour glass of our lives starts running out.

- This life is not a dress rehearsal. It is not a practice run. It is the real event. There is no 'take 2'. Every moment spent drifting, is a moment lost.

- Time is incredibly precious; it is the one thing you can give away which you can never get back.

- It is far better to live a life filled with quality time rather than quantity.

- People who have run out of time lament not spending more time doing the things most important to them; like spending time with loved ones, pursuing their passions and taking more risks.

- Successful people spend their time in distinctly different ways to unsuccessful people.

- One of the best ways to make your time more productive is to focus on your single most important purpose and stick to this with persistence and determination.

CHAPTER 2

Unleash the Awesome Power of Goals

"Set your own goals or someone else will set them for you, and you will probably not like what they have in mind for you to do".

David Barton

Do you have any goals? If you do, what are they? If you don't, don't worry because you soon will have some.

Most People Don't Have Goals

What is a goal? Simply speaking, a goal is an observable and measurable end result, which has one or more objectives to be achieved within a certain time frame.

As an author of a program on goal setting, I often engage in conversation with people about their goals. The reactions and feedback I get are both interesting and enlightening.

I have found that many people will say "yes" if they are asked if they have goals. However, when asked if those goals are written down and accompanied by written plans, most people say "no".

I am sorry to be the harbinger of bad news, but unless your goals are written down and accompanied by a plan, they are *not* goals. These 'goals' are just dreams, desires, fantasies or hopes.

So why do people say they have goals, when they don't commit and write them down?

I believe one of the most likely reasons is due to social conditioning. We have all been taught from birth that we need to be good, and live responsible lives. Goal setting happens to be a 'responsible thing' to do. Most of us want to do well and feel accepted and liked, so we tell ourselves and others that we have goals when in reality we don't.

Only 3% to 8% of People Set Goals

When you take a closer look at the global population, what you find is that only about 3% – 8% of people set goals, and systematically make plans to achieve them. The rest of the world simply engages in what author Napoleon Hill calls "wishful thinking".

Unfortunately, wishes do not turn into riches – if they did we would all be rich. The truth is that wealth, success, health, happiness, and every other thing you richly desire, can only be gained through establishing definite plans, backed by deliberate action, and pursued through constant persistence. Success doesn't happen by accident, it happens by design.

Research from the Statistics Brain at the University of Scranton showed that roughly 45% of Americans make New Year's resolutions. However, less than 50% of them achieve anything of note. Only about 8% of those who set New Year's Resolutions achieve their goals fully.[9] The reality is that a minority of Americans achieve their goals, while the majority fail.

One of the reasons I believe people fail so frequently at achieving their goals, is that they never had goals to achieve in the first place. All these people really had was a wish, desire, or fantasy.

Goal setting moves you out from the realm of wishful thinking, and into the domain of turning your wishes into targetable, concrete plans and realistically attainable purposes. Goal setting, when used properly, is one of the most important vehicles to help you achieve the dreams and desires you have always wanted, in a time frame faster than you ever thought possible.

This claim is not just pie in the sky conjecture. Decades of research into goal setting has shown that people who set goals are more productive, and effective in their jobs, than those who do not set goals. [55]

If you want to achieve more, be more productive, and turn your dreams into reality, you can. But, you might have to make some changes. For one, you will have to define what it is you want. Then, you will have to formulate goals, make plans for those goals, and systematically go about achieving them one day at a time, with persistence and self-discipline.

How To Use This Book

This book has been designed to help you turn your dreams into reality. This starts with the most important step; clarifying what it is you want the most out of life.

Before you decide what you want, you should know what it is that you truly value. Rather than scale the mountain of success to discover you were climbing the wrong mountain, this book will help you to uncover your most important values. This way, you can set the right goals, and pursue the dreams best for you. When you reach the summit of your mountain, it needs to be one aligned with your own internal beliefs and values.

Once you have achieved this important step, you will be ready to formulate your goals. During this process, you will also discover your most important objectives. These are the ones you should be spending most of your time and effort on. These are the goals which will provide you with the biggest reward; the goals which will make the greatest impact on your life if achieved today. At this point, you should also define your mission statement, which will help guide you and keep you on course as you move towards your desired destination.

Once you have your goals, you will be ready to plan and pursue them. This next step involves devising a plan to achieve your goals. Part of this plan involves you programming your subconscious mind with your goals, and devising ways to place these goals in the fore-front of your mind, as much as possible.

You will be shown how to use one of the most important tools this book has to offer: The Goal Achievers Journal. Using this journal is one of the best ways to input your goals into your mind, and activate your subconscious to go in pursuit of them.

The final 4 Chapters of this book involve developing key skills, which will help you accomplish your goals faster. For many people, these core skills will determine if they will get started on their goals, or just watch life drift by. So many dreams become unrealised, because, even though goals might get written down, they never get started. The skills of persistence, self-discipline, courage and overcoming procrastination are essential for people who have big goals and big dreams. Each one of these skills are discussed in more detail later in this book.

Why Should You Set Goals

Before we get ahead of ourselves, let's take a quick look at why goal setting is important, and answer some key issues:

- Why should you set goals?

- What are some of the reasons people fail to set goals?

- What are the benefits of goal setting?

Without goals you will go nowhere

In the classic Lewis Carroll story, Alice in Wonderland,[17] Alice came to a fork in the road.

Alice: "Which road do I take?"

Cheshire cat: "Where do you want to go?"

Alice: "I don't know."

Cheshire cat: "Then, it doesn't matter."

If you don't know your destination, then it doesn't matter which road you take, any road will do when you have no goal in mind. But, chances are that somewhere, will be nowhere.

The reality is, if you do not set your own goals, someone else will set them for you, and chances are you won't like what they have intended for you to do. Author Jim Rohm, said, "If you don't design your own life plan, chances are you'll fall into someone else's plan. And guess what they have planned for you? Not much."

All successful people take charge of their own destinies, and set goals and plans in motion, which direct their lives in the direction that they want to go. Successful people take responsibility for their own lives, and do not leave it to chance or in the hands of others, particularly others who do not have their best interests at heart.

Unfortunately, for one reason or another, most people simply drift through life, and leave the goal setting business to others to do for them. A poem by Jessie Rittenhouse called *My Wage*, he aptly describes the approach most people take with their lives.

I bargained with Life for a penny,
And Life would pay no more,
However I begged at evening
When I counted my scanty store.

For Life is a just employer,
He gives you what you ask,
But once you have set the wages,
Why, you must bear the task.

I worked for a menial's hire,
Only to learn, dismayed,
That any wage I had asked of Life,
Life would have willingly paid.

So what have you asked life for? Have you, like so many millions, just bargained with life for a menial days hire? In today's terms a menial days hire would be the equivalent of minimum wage, or maybe slightly better.

I have briefly worked in some companies, where I met several people who had been working there for 20 to 30 years, and they were still paid close to minimum wage. They had been working tirelessly, and faithfully, for those companies for the better part of their lives, and their hourly wage had only increased by a few cents or dollars.

But this was not by accident; for the majority of these people it was not some random consequence, or misfortune. Their situation had come about, because this was precisely what they bargained with life for. However, had they bargained with life for a whole lot more, life would have been happy to pay.

I believe this is precisely what happens in the real world. Successful people seem to have a natural talent for achieving big goals, but in reality, they bargained with life for much more, and got it. They were audacious enough to ask life for what they really wanted, and discovered life was only too willing to pay.

However, a far different reality transpires for millions of others. As I have unequivocally stated, most people do not set goals for themselves, but rather leave the goal setting for others to do for them. The end result is a life filled with regret, and unrealised dreams. When you leave the goal setting of your life for others to do, you are effectively bargaining with life for a penny, and life will pay you that penny, and still demand the same amount of effort it does of the people who ask it for a whole lot more.

So what are you going to bargain with life for today? Are you going to set the wage high or ask for a menial days hire? The truth is, that you still have time to get much more from life than you ever thought possible.

This Life Is The Real Event

Your life is not a practice run. It is the real event. If you want to leave this earth with no regrets, now is your only chance to make that happen. You will not get another chance. Your time is now.

However, when you do not take charge of your own life, someone else steps in, and assumes that role for you. They plot your course on a trajectory which is not your own. You end up spending your life working for them, and helping them achieve their dreams. In many cases, your goal ends up being the goal of making someone else rich; essentially helping someone else live the good life, while you get the scraps that fall off their table.

If you want more than just scraping by, and getting the left overs of others, you need to take the bull by the horns, and gain back the reins of your life! You need to define what it is you want, and then set your course to go out and get it.

This may not be easy, at least at first, as breaking old habits and beliefs can be tricky. Our beliefs can often get in the way of our success, because we may intentionally (or unintentionally) use various arguments to convince ourselves why we cannot do something.

Typical Reasons People Don't Set Goals

It has been estimated that about 95% of the world's population do not set goals, or establish plans to achieve them. Here are a few reasons why:

1. People don't set goals due to their *Fear*

There are three primary fears which can block goal setting. They are the fear of failure, fear of success and the fear of rejection. Let's consider each of these fears separately.

Fear of Failure

It is understandable why people might succumb to the fear of failure, particularly if pursuing their goal could cost them their life, house, family, or anything else they value highly. However, most people do not usually set goals that engage with this level of risk – like climbing Mt Everest without oxygen - so their fear is most likely more socially based.

Most people are more likely to fear jeers, laughs, snide remarks or 'told you so' comments from their social groups, family, friends and colleagues. These people take the safer route, and choose not to set goals that could attract other people's negative responses, in the event they happen to fail.

One way to deal with this fear is not to tell anyone about your goals until you have achieved some measure of them. If, for some reason, you don't achieve your goal, no one will be the wiser.

Failure to achieve is not the worst outcome. To not have tried is! Michael Jordan, says, "I've missed more than 9,000 shots in my career. I've lost almost 300 games. 26 times, I've been trusted to take the game winning shot and missed. I've failed over and over and over again in my life. And that is why I succeed."[46]

Like Michael Jordan, you can choose to embrace your fear of failure, making it a component of your success, rather than a factor to be avoided. The sooner and faster you can fail, the sooner you will succeed, because each successive failure is one step closer to success.

In his book *Awaken The Giant Within*,[65] author, speaker and life coach Anthony Robbins relates how he became such an excellent public speaker. At the beginning of his career he worked in an organisation where he promoted seminars for Jim Rohm. Rather than booking himself once per week like many of the others in the organisation, he booked himself 3 times per day. He spoke to anyone who would listen. The experience that others gained in forty-eight speaking engagements per year, he gained in two weeks. He greatly multiplied his learning rate and accelerated his success through a process of improving on his failures. Robbins says that not all his speeches were great, far from it, but he learnt from each delivery and improved on each speech. Soon he could walk into a room of any size and reach people from virtually any walk of life.

It has been said that Thomas Edison failed over 1,000 times when he developed the light bulb. Many people don't even attempt something once, never mind 1,000 times.

Fear of Success

As crazy as it sounds, some people fear success! They are afraid at what success might mean for them, what aspects of their lives will have to change, or how badly their comfort zones will be affected.

If you succeed, you may have to change the status quo, and live life differently. For example, if you succeeded financially, you might fear how others will perceive you, because you now have more money. Possibly, you fear others will expect more from you, and if you are unwilling to comply, will reject you. It is true that some things might have to change if you achieve more success, and you might not be comfortable, willing, or ready to make that change.

Fear of Rejection

Many people fear the rejection that might result from failing to achieve their goals, or even from achieving their goals..

The truth is, many of your friends, family, colleagues, and community will be envious of you, if you succeed. They might become jealous of your achievements; they might get angry, annoyed or frustrated that you are doing well, while they are left struggling to get ahead.

Should this stop you from pursuing your goals? Should you slink back into the shadows, because someone else might not be happy with you succeeding?

Author Jack Canfield said, "One of life's fundamental truths states, 'Ask and you shall receive.' As kids we get used to asking for things, but somehow we lose this ability in adulthood. We come up with all sorts of excuses and reasons to avoid any possibility of criticism or rejection".[15] Don't let the fear of rejection rob you of your opportunity to pursue your dreams.

2. People don't know how to set goals

Most schools either do not teach goal setting in the curriculum, or they do an inadequate job. If kids get poor instruction in goal setting, the result might be that they erroneously think they know how to set goals, when really they don't!

When you try and correct them, they bark at you, because teenagers apparently know everything. I know this being a father of teenagers myself. I believe most people grow up with a poor understanding of goal setting, and a lack of appreciation of the power of setting, and pursuing goals.

Confucius said, "Real knowledge is to know the extent of one's ignorance". If people don't know the importance of goal setting, as a component of personal success, then how can they implement the process?

We need to be careful with choosing the people with whom we associate, because the people we surround ourselves with may not be good role models of successful goal setting behaviour. People and places will not always support your goals. In their book, "Connected: The surprising power of social networks and how they shape our lives"[19] authors Christakis and Fowler state that if your close friend becomes obese, you are 57% more likely to become obese yourself. You become like the people you spend most of your time with.

The people we see tend to set the standards for what we consider appropriate. In a study reported in a social developmental journal, it was found that out of 500 school students, those who established relationships with high achieving students experienced improvements in their report cards. Those with high achieving friends benefited, in terms of their motivational beliefs and academic performance.

The message here is to seek out people who model good goal setting behaviour. Spend more time learning from them and they will help your success to sky rocket.

3. People don't think goals are important

Many people don't think goal setting is important, and it's easy to see why. We live in a world where the majority of people don't set goals, so you will seldom encounter another human being who continuously and consistently engages in the habit of setting and pursuing goals.

There is a large body of research which shows that we learn by mirroring other people's behaviours, attitudes and beliefs.[18, 44] Our brains contain specialised neurons called mirror neurons, which help us learn by replicating the behaviours of others. If the people around you don't set goals, then it makes sense that you will do likewise. If people around you don't believe goal setting is important, then it is likely you will develop these same attitudes and beliefs.

Of course, the most successful people in the world know the value of goal setting, which is why they are so successful. Successful people usually hang around people like themselves, who also value goal setting. Psychological literature is full of evidence that we are more attracted to people who are most similar to ourselves.[7, 14]

Considering your own upbringing and family background, have you developed the belief that setting and achieving goals are not important? Take a look around you, and see if the people you surround yourself with believe and share the same attitudes as you.

If you begin to develop a new mind-set, and modify your actions to become a goal setter, you will begin to influence those around you more positively. Your example will serve to encourage them to take action on their own dreams. They will likewise begin enjoying the benefits which result from establishing their own life plans, and setting targets which lead them towards a life they deeply desire.

4. They already think they have goals

Many people mistakenly believe they already have goals.

But, goal setting is a very specific activity which involves developing strategies, and directing behaviours towards achieving them. Setting goals is not something you just dream about now and then.

Setting goals is much more than just fantasizing or daydreaming. Poet, Robert Frost, said "A man will sometimes devote all his life to the development of one part of his body - the wishbone."

Unfortunately, the wishbone does not help someone get what they want. Wishing, daydreaming, and fantasising may for a slim moment make us feel good, but when you snap back into reality nothing will have changed and you will still be in the same place as you were before.

If you want to make a real difference in your life, you must go in pursuit of the dream, not just leave it to swirl around in your head. As Barbara Sher author of *I Could Do Anything If I Only Knew What It Was: How to Discover What You Really Want and How to Get It* said, "You must go after your wish. As soon as you start to pursue a dream, your life wakes up and everything has meaning."[74]

5. They are too lazy to be bothered

Goal setting requires effort, and many people would rather just blob in front of the television than work on their goals.

According to a recent survey,[64] New Zealanders watch television for an average of 2:48 hours a day, followed closely by Australians, with 2:40 hours a day. They spend just as much time on the internet.

Sitting around watching TV makes us lazy, and unlikely to pursue our goals. This is a global problem though, and not just indicative of New Zealand/Australian culture. Just imagine what you could achieve if you turned some of those wasted hours in front of the TV screen into productive hours pursuing your dreams.

Some studies suggest that extended periods watching television changes the anatomical structure of children's brains, and negatively impacts their verbal abilities. Although not conclusive, other studies suggest that watching loads of television leads to more antisocial behaviour, more mental health problems, and obesity.[66, 85, 87]

One of the primary problems with wasting so much of our lives in front of the screen is that it negatively impacts our intelligence. Our intelligence is left undeveloped, and we not only lose the countless hours we could be spending being productive, but we also decrease our cognitive performance.

I am not anti-watching television, movies or going to the cinema, but these behaviours should not take precedent over the more important things we could be engaging in.

The 8 Most Important Reasons Why You Should Set Goals

Now that we have covered some of the typical reasons people do not set goals, let's look at some of the reasons why we should. Goal setting has been the subject of extensive research in the fields of psychology, management and business. This research shows that goal setting practices have several benefits for individuals and businesses alike.

1. Goals help you set direction for your life

Goals help us find direction in life, which stops us drifting from one day to the next.

Hal Urban, author of *Life's Greatest Lessons*, said, "Living without goals is like going on a trip without a destination. If you don't know where you're going, you'll probably end up nowhere, and any road will get you there."[80]

Goals give us direction. They give us a track to run on, a path to follow, so we know where we are headed.

In 1952, Florence Chadwick became the first woman to attempt a solo swim of 26 miles between Catalina Island and the California coastline. As she attempted her journey, she was flanked by small boats which watched out for sharks, and were ready to support her in the event she grew tired or got into trouble.

After about 15 hours into her journey, thick fog descended all around her and she could no longer see very far in front of her and she lost her direction. She began to doubt that she could make it. She kept going for another hour before giving up and being pulled into a boat. Shortly after she discovered that she had given up just 1 mile from the Californian shore line; her destination.

Two months later, Florence attempted the feat again. This time however, she made the 26 mile trip in a straight path without defeat, even though the same thick fog once again descended on her and blocked her view of the coastline.

When she was asked how she had managed to complete the trip this time, Florence said that she created a mental image of the shoreline in her mind, and focused on the mental, rather than the actual image of her goal.

Florence teaches us an important lesson about goal setting. Like her, when you have your destination in sight, be that real or imagined, it becomes much easier to reach. Without it, you might lose hope and give up on your dreams.

2. Goals help you find your focus

Focus means following one course until successful. Goals help you focus your energy, time, and efforts into very specific areas of your life.

Just like we can harness the sun's diffused rays of sunlight, by focusing it through a lens onto a certain spot, so we can focus our attention onto very specific objectives. The result is a huge transfer of energy which can light a fire.

Focus is the opposite of multitasking. Research shows that we are not very good at multitasking. According to a recent study, humans do not do several tasks simultaneously; instead, we switch from one task to another very rapidly.[38] But, multitasking comes at a cognitive cost. By switching between tasks continuously, we reduce our performance and increase errors in what we do.

Focus achieves the complete opposite. When you focus on just one task at a time, you make it easier on your brain, which allows you to achieve your goals faster and more accurately.

Warren Buffet, most notably one of the world's greatest investors, is a big believer in the power of focus. He believes in the importance of remaining focused over time. Buffet says, "Successful investing takes time, discipline and patience. No matter how great the talent or effort, some things just take time: you can't produce a baby in one month by getting nine women pregnant."

3. Goals give you purpose

Goals give you purpose, and something to get up for in the morning. Charles Henry Parkhurst (1842-1933) an American Clergyman once said, "Purpose is what gives life a meaning."

If you want your life to have meaning, you need to find your purpose. When you have meaningful goals which are important to you, you create purpose. The fact is that most of the greatest successful people in the world are those with a clear purpose.

Bruce Lee's path to stardom was not initially paved with ease. His early days living in the USA were characterised by struggle and difficulty. One day, he decided to write a letter to himself: "By 1980, I will be the best known oriental movie star in the United States and will have secured $10 million dollars... and in return, I will give the very best acting I could possibly give every single time I am in front of the camera and I will live in peace and harmony."

Bruce Lee went on to become a huge success in the movie industry, until his unfortunate death in 1973. He made several blockbuster movies, including *Enter the Dragon*. Sadly, he died before the movie's release, from a rare sensitivity to certain painkillers. Several months later, the movie was released, and it was a huge global hit. Had he still been alive he would have gotten far more reward than what he had originally written to himself.

Having a clear purpose of what he wanted to achieve made the difference between Bruce Lee becoming an action hero superstar, or an actor who spent his days in obscurity.

4. Goals help you become more independent

Goals help you take charge of your life.

As Writer Henry David Thoreau says, "What you get by achieving your goals is not as important as what you become by achieving your goals".

What you become is the captain of your own ship, able to set course in the direction of your dreams. When you are independent, you become responsible for your own successes and take ownership of your failures.

If you don't set goals, you will be at the mercy of following other people's agendas; you will become enrolled into the ranks of the masses of willing, and unwilling participants who work on achieving other people's goals. In many cases you will be the latter; reluctantly following someone else's path and contributing to their success, whilst feeling like you have no choice other than to serve your master, as your own dreams and ambitions go unrealised.

Author Steven Covey says, "Every human has four endowments - self-awareness, conscience, independent will and creative imagination. These give us the ultimate human freedom... the power to choose, to respond, to change."[32]

Having your own goals, and working towards them will allow you to tap into the endowments which make life worth living. The ultimate human freedom is to express yourself creatively, and the only way you can truly realise this is to become someone who sets and pursues his or her own goals.

5. Having goals will help you work more efficiently

It has been said that in the absence of clearly defined goals, we become strangely loyal to performing daily acts of trivia.

When you have clearly defined goals, you gain a clearer understanding of what your most important tasks are. You garner a clearer picture of what your primary objectives should be, and when these are pursued you will save time, energy, frustration, stress, and money. By ignoring trivial tasks and concentrating on the important ones you will become more effective and efficient in your work.

Former British Prime Minister Benjamin Disraeli once said, "There can be economy only where there is efficiency." Efficiency gets the job done with less effort, time and resources. But without goals, you will wander in a mist of uncertainty, expending effort on frivolous pursuits, and achieving very little.

6. Having goals gives you hope

So many people live their lives without hope. They linger on their day to day activities in despair. Their future looks bleak, and they feel they have little chance of ever rising out of the dark hole they currently find themselves in.

The good news is that goal setting gives you hope for a better future, and for a happier tomorrow. For some people this will give them a new lease on life. A hope for a better future can be life transforming.

Dr Robert Schuller, a well-known evangelist, said that it was harder to raise $1,000 dollars to buy a new dishwasher, than it was to raise $1,000,000 for a "tower of hope".

This only makes sense if you realise that big goals inspire and stimulate people to action, because they foster a sense of hope in bigger and better things. Hope is a very powerful motivating force, capable of pushing people further than they ever thought they could go, beyond their wildest imaginings and past their perceived limitations.

Jim Carrey is another example of someone who had to overcome adversity and self-doubt before making it big in Hollywood. One night, after he had performed his stand-up comic routine in a Los Angeles night club, he got booed off the stage by the audience.

From the top of Mulholland Drive, he began to question if this was the life he wanted. Did the city hold his ticket to success or failure? He pulled out his cheque book and wrote himself a cheque for ten million dollars. He made a note on it, "For acting services rendered."

The cheque stayed in his wallet for a time. Eventually, Carrey would act in blockbuster comedies like *Dumb and Dumber*, but it was not until his role in *The Cable Guy* that he finally reached his dream. In fact he smashed through it. He got paid $20 million for this role, and at that time became the highest ever paid comedy actor in history.

Jim Carrey's story illustrates an important lesson about hope. Having hope can be the driving force keeping you on the road less travelled, while life throws all sorts of fiery troubles your way. For most people, these challenges will block and derail their efforts, but for someone who has well established goals, they will simply be a bump in the road to victory.

7. Having goals impacts your level of happiness positively

The Dalai Lama believes that the purpose of our lives is to be happy. Possibly you agree with this estimate of our life's purpose, or maybe you believe it is more than that, or something entirely different. What's important though, is that most people would agree they want to be happy. No one wants to be depressed or miserable in life, at least no one I know.

Author Henry David Thoreau says that, "Happiness is like a butterfly: the more you chase it, the more it will elude you, but if you turn your attention to other things, it will come and sit softly on your shoulder."

If you have ever been in a garden, among the flowers, and tried to catch a butterfly, you will understand what Thoreau means. The butterfly will escape your grasp and dodge your attempts to capture it. However, if you stand still, you will notice it will flutter close by, and maybe even rest on you for a moment.

This is somewhat similar to happiness. If you try to make happiness your goal, it will escape you. If you focus on doing things which impact your life positively, you will notice happiness will find you. Ben Sweetland said "happiness is a journey, not a destination, so turn your attention to doing other things and happiness will make a path to your door."

Below is a list of 'other things' you can do, which have been shown to increase happiness. The interesting thing about this list is that many of the items on it can be turned into actionable goals.

14 ways to increase your happiness

1. Take action on your goals.

2. Free your heart from hatred, and develop a profound ability to forgive.

3. Live more simply. We live in a highly materialised world where keeping up with the Jones' keeps us from living a simpler life.

4. Develop your faith, and build a close relationship with God.

5. Exercise more to boost your energy: 7 minutes per day could be enough to experience the positive benefits exercise gives.

6. Get the right amount of sleep to help boost your positive emotions.

7. Spend more time with real people. Put down the phone and get out and about with family, friends and colleagues.

8. Get outdoors more, and enjoy the sunshine and fresh air.

9. Be more generous with your time and help others. Some suggest 100 hours a year is the magic number.

10. Smile more. Try smiling more and notice how people smile back. Smiling is catchy, and is a big mood booster.

11. Plan a Trip. Even if you don't take the trip, the plan itself is a positive mood promoter.

12. Meditation can increase mood by training your mind to focus on positive thoughts, and expel negative ones.

13. Cut back your commute time. Move closer to work, or find a job closer to home.

14. Practice gratitude. Being more thankful increases your happiness and that of others too.

8. Having goals can increase your self-efficacy

Belief in oneself and having the confidence to achieve what you set your mind to do is a by-product of goal setting. When you set goals and repeatedly achieve them, you will develop an attitude that you can do anything you decide to do.

Setting and achieving your goals will boost your self-belief. But what if you lack belief in yourself, and are currently struggling to find the motivation to get yourself moving in the direction of your goals? Here are a few tips which can immediately increase your confidence, and improve your motivation to achieve your best dreams.

1. **Put on your best clothes and look sharp.** Your clothing can change the way you feel about yourself. Good quality clothing can make you feel more confident and positive. One great rule to follow when buying clothes is: spend twice as much, and buy half as much. Thus, you will buy better looking, quality clothes in less quantity. The bonus is less clutter in your closet.

2. **Walk Faster.** This might sound like a silly idea, but researchers have studied the relationship between walking faster and confidence. Walking faster makes you feel more confident and onlookers view you as more important and confident.

3. **Sit in the front row.** People often try and sit in the back row, but this leaves the impression of lack of self-confidence. Trying to hide away in the back is probably not the best route to take when you want more self-confidence. It sends the wrong message to others, and most importantly to you. People with high levels of self-confidence sit in the front row and are not afraid of being noticed. They ask questions, and make comments without fear of ridicule or rejection.

4. **Work out, build muscle and get fitter**. This will make you look more physically confident, and also make you feel good about yourself. Have you ever noticed how elite athletes move about? They seem to carry themselves with a sense of power. They walk upright, head held high. They

don't slouch or cower. There is a lot to be gained by being physically conditioned and strong.

5. **Leave your comfort zone, and step out into new territory.** Take a risk, and do something new. Take on a new challenge.

6. **Be yourself.** We live in a world beset by social conditioning. We are constantly being bombarded with messages and instructions on how to be, what to think and how to behave. In a world like this, it's hard to know who you are, and what you stand for. It is even harder when you lack confidence. Jack Canfield said, "self-acknowledgment and appreciation are what give you the insights and awareness to move forward toward higher goals and accomplishments."

Albert Bandura once said, "self-belief does not necessarily ensure success, but self-disbelief assuredly spawns failure".

KEY POINTS TO REMEMBER

- Most people who set goals at the beginning of the year fail to achieve them.

- The majority of the world's population do not formally declare to themselves (and others) what they truly want out of life. They do not set meaningful goals for themselves; choosing instead to maintain the status quo, and achieve the minimum with their lives. They do very little other than fantasise, daydream and wish upon a star, when it comes to what they truly desire.

- Many people don't know what they want, and have never really taken out the time to plot their own course and set their own goals. They end up just drifting from one day to another, year after year until it's too late.

- Most people leave the job of setting major goals to others to do for them, and then spend their lives achieving someone else's dream. If you don't set goals for your own life, someone else will set them for you. There is no choice in the matter; you either live your life fulfilling your own dreams, or you live it fulfilling someone else's.

- People use several reasons to justify why they are reluctant to formally establish meaningful goals for their lives. None of these reasons are valid and are really just excuses used to hide behind one or another fear, or inclination for not taking action.

- Goal setting has many benefits, and has been the subject of extensive scientific research over the decades. Evidence is clear that goal setting, and pursuit, results in being more productive, efficient and effective. People who set goals achieve more, and gain greater success than those who do not.

CHAPTER 3

Capturing Your Desires, and Defining What You Want

"If you feel like there's something out there that you're supposed to be doing, if you have a passion for it, then stop wishing and just do it."

Wanda Skyes

Before you get down to the process of goal setting, formulating plans, and starting the step by step process of achieving your dreams, it is important to know what it is that you want in life.

The simple truth is that knowing what you want is not always obvious. Gaining clarity about your best dreams and greatest desires is not as easy as you might think.

Therefore, the start of the goal setting process involves taking some time to explore the many aspects of your life in which you would like to achieve something important.

Knowing what is most important to you is probably the most significant component of goal setting, because it establishes your focus and gives you your direction. Without clarity about what you want, you will simply remain wandering in the wilderness of uncertainty, wasting your precious time like sand sifting through an hour glass.

The key objective of this Chapter is to take you on a journey of self-discovery. Through this journey, you will become more aware of what you want to achieve with your life.

In this Chapter you will use several tools, and will do several exercises to help you uncover your dreams, desires, beliefs and values. This will form the foundation onto which you will then build your goals.

Take your time to complete this Chapter. Don't rush the process. Think deeply about what you want. It may take several days to uncover your most important objectives and priorities. This is not a race, there are no prizes for getting through this process faster than you need to. Clarity is the goal, and finding clarity takes time.

THE POWER OF FOCUS

One of the defining attributes of successful people is that they have laser-like focus.

We all face distractions in our daily lives, but the ability to filter out useless, unimportant and inconsequential interruptions is what separates the great achievers from the mediocre actors. Focus is a skill which ignites productivity, by keeping you on target and enabling you to achieve your highest goals over a sustained period of time.

In Warren Buffett's biography, *The Snowball,*[70] writer Alice Schroeder retells of an event when Buffet goes to a dinner party on a Fourth of July holiday. Bill Gates also happened to be present. During dinner, Gates posed a question, "What factor was the most important in getting to where they had gotten in life?" Buffet answered, "Focus", and Gates concurred. For both

Buffet and Gates, focus was the key that unlocked the door to their considerable success.

Become A Specialist

One of the great secrets to living a successful life is to become a specialist, not a generalist; to develop the skills of a sniper, and not a machine gunner. This is the ability to give all of your attention, unequivocally, to a very specific, and defined target, and to stick at it with self-discipline and persistence.

Richard St John, author of the book, The *8 Traits Successful People Have in Common*,[75] believes that success is, "narrowing down and focusing on one thing, not being scattered all over the map." St. John says that according to Buffett, putting money in a lot of things is "a Noah's Ark way of investing - you end up with a zoo that way."

Dr Dennis Waitley, author of *The Psychology of Winning*, said, "success is almost totally dependent upon drive, focus and persistence."[82] Anyone can develop those three qualities, so anyone can be successful at whatever they decide to do. Success is not limited to certain types of people, born on the right side of the tracks. Goal achievement is the right of every human being on the planet.

Anyone can achieve success at their goals

Many people may object and say that they are too old, young, not mentally or physically capable, not intelligent enough, or from the wrong background. But, reality strongly contradicts that objection.

There is no particular 'type' of person more capable of success than others. Through the examples that follow, I hope you will agree with me that it does not depend on age, culture, gender, race, physical and mental health, or intelligence, to do great things with your life.

Age

Take Japanese born, Yuichiro Miura, who just before his 81st birthday successfully reached the summit of Mt Everest, making him the oldest man on earth to achieve this amazing feat of human endurance.

Another extraordinary example is Harriette Thompson, a cancer survivor, who on the 31st of May 2015, at the age of 92 completed the San Diego Marathon in well under 8 hours. This feat made her the oldest woman in the world to achieve this goal. Another example is 101 year old Fauja Singh, who in 2013 at the ripe old age of 101, finished the Hong Kong 10km running event in 1hour, 32 minutes and 28 seconds.

Age did not appear to be a factor for Frank Schearer, who at 101 was the world's oldest water skier. Another example is Harland David Saunders, who at age 65 started KFC, now a multi-billion dollar global corporation. This is one end of the age spectrum, but we find similar astounding feats on the younger end too.

For example, at Age 1, child prodigy Christian Fredrich Heinecken, was purported to have read the first 5 books of the Bible (the Pentateuch). Olympic Skating Champion, Bonnie Blair began skating at age 2, while 9 year old Daisy Ashford wrote a bestselling novel, The Young Visiters, which sold over 200,000 copies (quite a feat for any author at any age).

Age does not have the market on success. These few examples are of people on the edges of the age life scale (very young and very old), but there are countless examples of other people in between who have achieved resounding success with their lives.

Mental Health

Mental health is another factor which does not predict success. Take for instance actors Catherine Zeta-Jones (Bipolar II disorder), Ashley Judd (depression and an eating disorder) and Jim Carrey (Bipolar disorder) who have all achieved remarkable success, in spite of their difficulties.

Likewise, President Abraham Lincoln (ADHD) and Prime Minister Winston Churchill (Depression) overcame similar difficulties. Buzz Aldrin, the astronaut who walked on the moon, struggled with depression and alcohol addiction, while Isaac Newton a world renowned scientist had an anxiety disorder.

Talent

Some people may cite lack of talent as their reason for lack of personal success. However, Henry Ford may object. Most people would have thought of Henry Ford as a big failure who lacked talent for anything great. The reason was that his first few businesses failed miserably, and left him broke 5 times, before he founded the Ford Motor Company. He became one of the richest men on earth, and employed thousands of people to build his motor cars.

Likewise, Walt Disney was not an immediate success. In the early days of his working life he was fired from his job at a newspaper by the editor who said, "He lacked imagination and had no good ideas." Following that, his first few businesses also ended in abject failure. Today, his movies and theme parks brighten up the lives of millions.

Albert Einstein didn't speak until he was 4, and did not read until he was 7. His parents and teachers thought he was mentally handicapped, slow and antisocial. He eventually won a Nobel Prize and changed the face of modern physics.

Thomas Edison also struggled at school in his early years. Teachers said he was, "too stupid to learn anything." He was fired from his first two jobs for not being productive enough. He went on to invent the light bulb, and lit up the world.

Winston Churchill struggled at school and failed 6th grade. He faced many years of political failure but finally became Prime Minister of the United Kingdom at the age of 65. He went on to win a Nobel Prize.

Oprah Winfrey went through a rough and abusive childhood. In her early career she struggled, and was fired from her job as a reporter for being, "unfit for TV." Today she is a billionaire and global TV personality.

During his first screen test, Actor Fred Astaire was told by the director, "Can't act. Can't sing. Slightly bald. Can dance a little." He went on to become a world renowned singer, dancer and actor.

Painter Vincent Van Gogh completed over 800 works in his lifetime, but only ever sold 1 to a friend and for not much money. He struggled for years, plugging away tirelessly, often starving himself. Today his work is worth hundreds of millions.

Stephen King had his first book "Carrie" rejected by 30 publishers, which caused him to give it up and throw it in the trash. His wife took it out and encouraged him to try once more. It got published, and today he is one of the most successful writers of our time.

Michael Phelps also overcame personal difficulties and has become a celebrated success. As a child, Michael Phelps was diagnosed with ADHD. His kindergarten teacher told his mom, "He's not gifted. Your son will never be able to focus on anything." His childhood coach, Bob Bowman, said that Michael spent a lot of time over by the life guard stand for disruptive behaviour.[48]

At times, some of this disruptive behaviour has cropped up from time to time in his adult life. Yet, Phelps has set dozens of world records. In 2004, at the Athens Olympic Games, he won 6 gold and 2 bronze medals, surpassing the legend Mark Spitz. Phelps currently holds the all-time record for Olympic gold medals at 23 gold. In total he has 28 medals.

From the age of 14, through to the Beijing games, Phelps trained 7 days per week, 365 days per year. He figured that if he trained Sundays too, he would get a 52 day advantage over the competition. He would spend up to 6 hours per day in the pool.[48] He focused all his energy into a one single discipline. Phelps became a person of selected discipline, and by doing so, demonstrated the practical outcome of doing what Inventor Alexander Bell said, "Concentrate all your thoughts upon the work at hand. The sun's rays do not burn until brought to a focus."

One thing you might notice about all the examples cited above, is that they all had a single focus. They all chose a specialty to put their time, energy and resources into. They all faced hardships and failure, but in the end they all made significant achievements.

How To Find Your <u>Focus</u>

For many people, focus does not simply fall into their laps. Most of us will have to go out and look for it. Many even experiment with several professions before deciding which one fits them best.

Personally, I believe that most people yearn to find their focus or purpose, and they hunger for some insight into what their role is; why they were put here on earth, and what they are meant to be doing with their lives. This is a recurring theme, and one which has attracted much attention of authors, speakers, preachers, movie makers and musicians.

Recently, I had a quick look at how many web pages were indexed by Google on the various search terms related to purpose, focus and meaning. The results showed that an astonishing 1 billion pages referenced the word "purpose", 123 million pages, "meaning of life", 1.2 billion pages "focus", and "what is my focus in life" found 405 million pages. A search on Amazon's database for books on the subject of "purpose of life" returned 234,134 results, and "meaning of life" gave 196,828 results. There is no doubt in my mind that finding focus, purpose, and meaning in life is one of the most important questions people seek to answer.

To start the process of discovering your focus, it pays to know what you are passionate about. If you know what you love doing, what you enjoy spending your time on, and what gives you the most enjoyment in life, you will be better able to find your focus.

PASSION: DO WHAT YOU LOVE

The word passion means to have an intense desire or enthusiasm for something. Passion also refers to love, fervour, preoccupation, and eagerness. Taken together, when you have a passion for something, it means you have a love for it. Passion gets you up in the morning, rearing to go. Does this describe your approach to the new day?

Many of the people St. John interviewed for his book, *The 8 traits successful people have in common,* said they loved what they did. Steve Jobs, for instance, said "I found what I loved to do early in life. Woz and I started Apple in my parent's garage when I was 20." Golf superstar, Tiger Woods, said "I absolutely love it. I love hitting the golf ball" and J.K Rowling, author of Harry Potter books, said, "I love writing these books. I don't think anyone could enjoy reading them more than I enjoy writing them."

Having a love for what you do is one of the key ingredients to achieving great success. Successful people are passionate about their goals. They know that to achieve great success will only happen when they truly love what they do.

According to St. John, there are two types of people: strivers and seekers.[75] Strivers know what they want from an early age, and go after it straight away. Most people are seekers, and need to spend time searching for their passion first. One way to determine if you have found your passion is to ask yourself 'Would I do it for free?' If you answer 'yes', then congratulations, you have found your passion. If your answer is 'no', then don't give up, keep on looking.

Filmmaker James Cameron (Titanic), Paul McCartney (Beatles), homemaking celebrity Martha Stewart, and evangelist Billy Graham were seekers, but when they eventually found their passion, they excelled in their chosen field. So if you haven't found your passion yet, don't worry, keep looking, because you still have time to make your mark on life.

How To Find Your Passion

Your passion won't simply drop into your lap or one day show up on your doorstep. Ken Mattingly, a veteran astronaut, and Apollo 13 hero, said "The more experiences and the faster you get 'em the better. They always pay off." He suggests that you need to experience life to uncover what it is you love. Do as much as you can, and take your opportunities to try new things. You may have to walk down many paths before you find the one you love.

Many successful individuals had to do the same; Albert Einstein was one of them. He worked as a patent clerk while he wrote 4 of his most important papers in his spare time. He didn't know from the offset what his passion was. Albert Einstein once said, "I have no special talents. I am only passionately curious." He pursued what he loved, and changed the face of physics.

When seeking out your passion, it is important to follow your heart, and not your wallet. Bill Gates (Microsoft) now the richest man in the world (2016) said, "Paul and I, we never thought we would make much money out of the thing. We just loved writing software." Similarly, Michael Jordan said, "I play the game because I love it. I just happen to get paid." These people didn't go after the money, they went after their passion. The money came later.

Jerry White, a professor of entrepreneurial studies at the University of Toronto said, "People whose only objective is making money, usually don't." He went on to say that you should find a product or service you can passionately believe in because without this you will not succeed.[47] If you don't love the product or service you are trying to sell, then find something you can love.

Napoleon Hill, author of the best seller "Think and Grow Rich", said that you don't have to be a fortune teller to predict someone's future. Hill said you simply have to ask one simple question: "What is your one definite purpose for your life – and what plans have you made to attract it?"

According to Hill, almost 98 out of 100 people will say something like, "I would like to earn a good living and be as successful as I can." On the surface of it, this seems like a reasonable answer, but dig a little deeper and you will find a drifter who will not go on to achieve anything of significance in life, other than the odd left over from truly successful people – who do have a definite purpose and a plan to attain it. [41]

If you want good things to be attracted into your life, you need to have a definite purpose (a single focus), and a plan to achieve it. How can anything be attracted to you, if you do not know what it is yourself? How can anyone offer you their help, if you don't know what you are trying to achieve?

Exercise 1

Here are a few questions you can ask yourself to uncover some of the passions you have.

1. What are you really good at doing?

2. What did you really enjoy doing as a child?

3. Would you still do what you currently do if you had to do it for free?

4. Complete this statement, "If I had no possibility of failing and my success was guaranteed I would. . ."

5. If you looked back 20 or 30 years from now what would you like to have achieved or accomplished?

DREAMS AND DESIRES

Another way to help you uncover your focus is to take an account of your dreams and desires. What do you fantasise about? What dreams take you off to another place and time? Where do you go when you get that dazed look on your face and the person talking to you says, "did you hear a word I just said?" We all have them. We all get dragged away by them. For some of us, we realise some of them. For others, we let them go unfulfilled.

Don't despise dreams and don't undervalue their worth. The journey to anything great starts with a dream; a bigger house, nicer car, happy family, loving partner, fluffy pets, plush carpet, diamond studded bracelets, the latest Smartphone.

Dreams come in all shapes and sizes and each person has their own unique picture of what they want in life. Our dreams may share similarities, but essentially they are our unique version of our ideal life.

In this section, we will consider ways to make your dreams more concrete. Unless you make your dreams more tangible, they will just remain incorporeal. They will simply stay in your head and never become reality.

Mind Mapping

One powerful technique you can use to capture your dreams is to use what Tony Buzan invented in the 70s, called Mind Mapping.[13] It is a useful technique, and helps you collect and organise information. Mind mapping appears to build on a cognitive model of the brain, which describes how it stores and organises information. This model is known as spreading activation.

For example, a single word is not just isolated in the brain, and disconnected from other words. Sounding one word will trigger thousands of other concepts which are associated to it. Your brain is a vast interconnected mass of neurons, joined together through synaptic connections. As one neuron fires, it triggers millions of others to fire as well.

The way neurons are connected in the first place is through association; related bits of information connected to each other, to form a network of related concepts.

A mind map therefore represents a similar relationship to the way your brain connects information. It is a diagram which represents related and connected ideas, thoughts, concepts, and images, all arranged around a central concept.

Research has shown that mind maps can increase productivity, most notably with people who are visual thinkers, but most people find the use of mind maps rewarding and helpful.

Mind Mapping Your Desires

Mind maps are excellent tools to help you capture your dreams, and discover the full range of everything you desire. You can choose to draw your mind map by hand, or use software to create larger maps. Software drawn maps are easier to rearrange, and to add other digital media to the map, like pictures and videos.

There are a number of software mind mapping tools you can use to create your mind maps. Most companies offer a limited free version, and paid versions with varying degrees of bells and whistles. Browse online, and you will discover a lot of them. I suggest you try them out and see which one works for you before going onto a paid version. Here are a few to get you started.

1. **Mind42** - www.mindmup.com

2. **Bubblus**- www.bubbl.us

3. **Mindomo** - www.mindomo.com

4. **MindMeister** - www.mindmeister.com

Guidelines On Making Your Mind Map

Be as specific as possible

Drill right down to the specifics of what you want. For example, if you want a particular car; state the model, colour, and if it has a tow bar, roof rack, rims, type of seat covers, and tinted windows. The more detail the better. It is fun to dream, and when you start to think about the details, you will find your excitement levels begin to rise.

Practice no limits thinking

Don't worry about desires that seem contradictory, just add them to the map at this stage. Contradictions will resolve themselves as you progress. Just let the creative juices flow, and don't worry how you will achieve any of these goals. This exercise is designed to capture what you want to have in life if you absolutely could not fail; if there were no limitations imposed on you at all. After a while, you will notice that you will run out of things that you desire, as the list is finite and not endless; there is a limit to what you want in life.

As content grows, rearrange you map

The power of the mind map is to create an organised associated network of your thoughts, so that you end up with major ideas, which shoot out branches of related concepts. This helps you to organise your thoughts into a cohesive and organised structure.

Periodically review your map

Mind maps are not static, and as you change so do they. As you achieve your goals, you can tick them off on your mind map. Soon, you will have many ticks to motivate and encourage you to achieve more and more of your goals.

Creating mind maps is a very useful method to capture your desires and dreams. For people who are more visual thinkers, this may be one of the best methods to use.

THE ROLES YOU PLAY

Another way to capture very specific goals is to consider the many roles you play in life. Our lives are multifaceted, and encompass many different roles. For instance, during my lifetime I have been a husband, father, brother, friend, colleague, student, athlete, writer, musician, cousin, nephew, grandson, employee, and employer. You can consider your goals for each of these roles, such as:

Role	Goals for each role
Husband	I will take my wife out once per week for diner/lunch.
Father	I will take each of my children out individually once per month to do something special like go to the movies or lunch.
Friend	I will go out for coffee once per month with each of my 3 good friends.

Writer	I will write 2000 words per day Mon to Friday first thing in the morning.
Athlete	I will train to run a 21km half marathon in 6 months in a time less than 2 hours.
Son	I will call/visit my parents at least once per week for at least 30 minutes per call/ or for 2 hours per visit.

Now it's your turn. What are your roles and what goals would you like to achieve for each:

ROLES	MY GOALS FOR EACH ROLE

Uncovering Your Greatest Dreams And Desires

In the next section you will be presented with several exercises, all designed to tap into your desires and dreams. Please take your time to complete these exercises with as much detail as possible.

The more detail you can provide now will produce greater clarity concerning your most important and highest goals. You can use mind maps as you capture your thoughts and ideas for most of this section.

Before you begin, get yourself a workbook, or pad of paper and complete each exercise on a new page.

Exercise 2: You Have Won $5 Million

You have just won a big prize, with certain conditions attached. What would you buy with this money? Make a list of anything you can buy with this money. The conditions are as follows: You are not allowed to invest this money, buy shares, put into bank or similar activities. You cannot give away the money to friends, family, or whoever, gift it or give it to charity. It has to be spent for products or services that you truly desire the most.

Exercise 3: You Got The Top Job

Overnight, there has been a significant change in your company. The company has decided to place you as the top managing director, or CEO. You are now in charge of the company. How would you lead the company? What strategy would you follow? What products or services do you want your company to offer? Where do you see your company in 5 or 10 years, with you in charge? How will the company grow and benefit by following your lead?

DREAM BOARDS

Dream boards are an excellent way to represent your dreams and desires. Dream boards are also known as vision boards, treasure maps, or vision maps. They are easy to produce, and you can use a ready supply of colourful and stimulating material from magazines, newspapers, advertising material, Google images, etc.

A dream board is a visual representation of your dreams. If you want to visit a tropical paradise, or own a particular luxury sedan, simply find photographs of these places and objects and paste them onto a board, into a journal, or you can even use software to search and find images online and create a collage.

There are several options to create your own dream board:

1. You can use traditional cut and paste techniques to stick photographs on a board (card board, cork board, white board). You can source the images online and print them, or use cut outs from magazines or other print media.

2. You can use computers and digital images to create a composite montage, and then print this instead. For instance, you can search for images online and save them to your Pinterest account (see www. Pinterest.com). Then you can arrange them the way you like. Alternatively, you can download Google's Picasa application, which allows you to create a collage from the images stored on your computer. You can then print this image as a JPG file to hang up on your wall, where you can continually be reminded of what you want in life. There are also free online applications, which allow you to create a collage of images. Do a search on Google for 'online vision/dream board creator' and you will find a number of alternatives.

3. You can also use the modern mind mapping software previously discussed as most programs allow you to import

media and attach them to your branches. You can print your mind map images later as a single image.

Exercise 4: What's on your Dream Board

On a separate page in your workbook or journal, paste images which represent your most important goals and desires. Look at them daily. Visual stimuli are very powerful, so your dream board will be an effective means to input your highest goals and desires into your subconscious mind.

YOUR VALUES

Your values are what make you, you. They are your most important beliefs, convictions, attitudes, ideals and expectations. Who you are, and what you do, is determined by your values. The problem is, most people are confused about their values, and consequently go on to produce very little with their lives. The good news is that the more clarity you have about your values, the more you will achieve.

Stephen Covey said, "Be sure that, as you scramble up the ladder of success, it is leaning against the right building". Make sure you are trying to scale the ladder that's right for you. The best way to achieve this is to gain clarity about your values.

Values are different from goals. For example, you might have a goal of getting your children up and ready for school on time, which sits within the value of being a **good parent.** You might have a goal of getting an A on your next assignment, which might sit within the value of **working hard**, or you might have a goal of going for a run 3 times per week, which sits within the value of **being healthy.**

Your values also have priority. You might give up your morning run if you suddenly get a call from your boss who demands you get to work early. The value of keeping your job overrides your value of personal fitness. However, you might tell your boss to take a hike if your spouse was admitted to hospital suddenly that morning. You prioritise your time and efforts based on your values. The values you hold most dear are the ones which will prevail when the crunch comes.

When your goals are based on your most important values, their attainment will leave you feeling more fulfilled when you finally achieve them. The inverse will most likely occur when your goals are not aligned with your values, as this will leave you feeling empty and dissatisfied when you reach your goals.

Define Your Core Values

Most people have never really taken out the time to consider what their core values are. It is very difficult to suddenly know what your values are in the spur of the moment, if you have not reflected on this aspect of your life much before.

Usually, these deep issues require some time and contemplation to unravel. My suggestion is that you take your time pondering the questions and exercises in this section. Think over your answers and don't rush the process. It could take several days for you to notice what your core values are.

Don't be afraid to change your answers after a few days. As you begin to unfold and explore the deeper workings of your mind, spirit and existence, new revelations will begin to emerge.

Below are a couple of tips to guide you as you work through the process of working out your core values.

Tip 1: Look At Your Actual Behaviour

As you begin to unravel your core values, regularly look and notice what your actual behaviours are, as you can't hide from what you do.

How many times have you said one thing, but did another? On one hand, you might claim to hold a certain belief, while on the other, your actions betray you.

We all have a public, and a private face. Our public face tries to make us look good in the eyes of others, but our private face tells a whole other story when we are alone. We are socially conditioned from birth to believe and say the right thing when we are in company, but really deep down, we don't believe these things at all. We are good at protecting our fragile self-esteems even if it means lying to ourselves and others.

My advice is to take a good, hard look at your actions to make a more honest assessment of your values. Actions really do speak louder than words. The truth will reveal itself when you are alone and no one is watching.

If you say you value health, then how often do you go out and exercise? How often do you eat junk food, drink alcohol or smoke?

If you say you value respect for others, then how often are you late and leave others waiting?

If you say you value family and friends, then how much time do you spend doing fun things together and taking time off work to just hang out?

If you say you value your parents, then how often do you call them or pay them a visit?

If you say you value your children, then how often do you spend quality time with them, take them out 1 on 1, or make time to watch them play their school sports?

What you do when presented with these real life situations will reveal your true values, and the priority they have in your life.

Tip 2: Evaluate Your Rationalisations and Excuses

You might hold a belief that one of your core values is family; that nothing else is more important to you than your family. You might also hold the belief that success is very important to you, but that success comes second to family.

However, most days you arrive home when your children are in bed asleep, and you leave early in the morning to go back to work before they are awake. You hardly ever see them, and what's more, you never purposely make time to spend with them.

You defend this behaviour by insisting you work hard for your family, so you can provide for their shelter, food, education and other needs. This may be true, but when you evaluate your values, from your children's point of view it might be hard to argue that you value them above your work. Let's face it, you tend to spend much more time at work, and hardly any time with them.

When you look beyond the veil of your rationalisations and excuses, you will discover your core values. If you ask your family, friends and colleagues what they think you value, you may be surprised.

The upcoming exercises are designed to help you uncover some of your most important values. The exercises are also designed to help you prioritise your values, according to their importance.

To uncover your core values, begin by asking yourself these questions:

1. What do you want to be remembered for?
2. When they read out your eulogy one day, what will they say about you?

3. If you asked your friends and family to describe you, what would they say?

4. Who are your most important role models? What do you admire about them?

5. What upsets you or makes you angry?

6. Think about someone you don't like. What traits do you not like about this person?

7. What kind of reputation do you have today?

8. Think about a situation recently when you were placed in a difficult position, and had to react under pressure. How did you react?

9. What do you want to be famous for?

10. What do you want to own, be, or do more than anything else in life?

Your 8 Most Important Values

Look at your answers to the previous questions, and list your 8 most important values in Table 1 below. Sometimes people really struggle to find the right words to describe their values, so to help you find the right words you can use Table 3 to assist you. Table 3 is a list of common values. It is by no means exhaustive, so you may think of other more appropriate words to describe your values not listed there. Have a read through the list and circle the items which you think describe your most important values.

Table 1: Core Values List

Your 8 most important values	
1.	2.
3.	4.
5.	6.
7.	8.

Prioritising Your Values

Starting from **item 1 in Table 1**, compare **item 1** to **item 2**. Which of these 2 values is the most important to you? Put a small tick next to the most important value.

Now compare **item 1** to **item 3** and decide which item (1 or 3) is more important to you. Put a tick next to the most important item like before. Continue in a similar vein, comparing item 1 to the other 5 items one at a time – each time putting a tick next to the most important item. When you have compared **item 1** to all the **items**, move to **item 2** and follow the process all over again. However, you don't need to compare item 2 to item 1 again as you have already done this. Simply compare item 2 to the items below it. When you are finished, you should have compared each item to all the other items in the table.

Count the number of ticks and record the number next to each item. Once you have counted the ticks next to each item you will have determined the order of importance for your top 8 values (If the same number of ticks exists for more than one item, which sometimes happens, simply compare the two and decide which is more important). Transfer this order to Table 2 in their order of importance. Write the value with the highest number in position 1 on the table. Continue to position 2, etc.

Table 2: The Order of Your Most Important Values

The Order of Your Most Important Values	
1.	2.
3.	4.
5.	6.
7.	8.

Table 3

Accountability	Discipline	Humorous	Respectful
Accuracy	Discretion	Independence	Restraint
Achievement	Diversity	Ingenuity	Results-oriented
Adventurous	Dynamism	Inner Harmony	Rigor
Altruism	Economy	Innovative	Security
Ambition	Educated	Inquisitiveness	Self-actualization
Assertiveness	Effectiveness	Insightfulness	Self-control
Athletic	Efficiency	Inspiring	Selflessness
Balance	Elegance	Intellectual Status	Self-reliance
Being the best	Empathy	Intelligence	Sensitivity
Belonging	Enjoyment	Intuition	Serenity
Boldness	Enthusiasm	Joy	Service
Calmness	Equality	Justice	Shrewdness
Carefulness	Excellence	Leadership	Simplicity
Challenge	Excitement	Legacy	Soundness
Cheerfulness	Expertise	Love	Speed
Clear-mindedness	Exploration	Loyalty	Spontaneity
Commitment	Expressiveness	Marriage	Stability
Community	Fairness	Mastery	Strategic
Compassion	Faith	Merit	Strength
Competitiveness	Family	Motivated	Structure
Consistency	Fidelity	Nurturing	Success
Contentment	Fitness	Obedience	Support
Continuous Improvement	Fluency	Open-minded	Teamwork
Contribution	Focus	Openness	Temperance
Control	Freedom	Optimistic	Thankfulness
Cooperation	Fun	Order	Thoroughness
Correctness	Generosity	Originality	Thoughtfulness
Courageous	Goodness	Passionate	Timeliness
Courtesy	Grace	Perfection	Tolerance
Creativity	Growth	Piety	Traditionalism
Curiosity	Happiness	Positivity	Trustworthiness
Decisiveness	Hard Work	Practicality	Truth-seeking
Democraticness	Health	Preparedness	Understanding
Dependability	Helping Society	Professionalism	Uniqueness
Determination	Holiness	Prudence	Unity
Devoutness	Honesty	Quality	Usefulness
Diligence	Honor	Reliability	Virtuousness
	Humility	Resourcefulness	Vibrant

KEY POINTS TO REMEMBER

- The most successful people in the world agree that focus is one of the most important keys to success in life. The ability to focus on a single endeavour, over a sustained period of time, is a critical factor in achieving your highest goals and grandest dreams.

- People who have clear focus also pursue what they love. They have a deep passion for their work, and are motivated each day to get up and get busy doing what they love. Unlike most people, they don't get out of bed reluctantly to go to work. They follow their hearts and have developed clear definite purposes for their lives. They make detailed plans to achieve their dreams and don't leave these important issues to chance.

- To gain clarity about your most important goals and deepest desires, you need to assess your dreams. They provide you with a rich source of information about what you want to have, achieve, and be in life.

- We all have a variety of roles to play in life. Our lives are multi-faceted. Each of our roles requires different goals. We can devise several important goals by considering our roles.

- Our values are important indicators of who we are and what we believe. What we do is a better indicator of our values than what we say. We need to have clarity on our values if we hope to set fulfilling and relevant goals. Lack of clarity here will likely result in us achieving goals which are hollow victories and empty accomplishments.

CHAPTER 4

Goal Formulation

"Stop setting goals. Goals are pure fantasy unless you have a specific plan to achieve them".

Stephen Covey

In the previous chapter I showed you why it is important to set goals. By doing the exercises, you will have defined what you truly desire, and uncovered some of your most important values.

Don't worry if you are not completely sure about any of these factors yet. It can take weeks, months even, to get a true understanding of your values and what it is you truly desire in life.

Some people spend years in therapy, and a small fortune trying to get to grips with who they are. In most cases, they come away with more insight but no actual solutions to their problems. In a sense this is an important reason why you should learn how to cultivate the art of goal setting. Rather than just talking about your problems, you take measurable steps to solving them.

In this chapter you will learn how to formulate actionable goals. You will learn about a very useful method to formulate and set achievable goals. It is a tried and tested method which will greatly improve your chances of getting what you want in life.

The method I am talking about is known as the SMART goal setting method. The general consensus regarding the SMART acronym, is that it was first written down in November 1981 in Spokane, Washington. A consultant named George Doran had published a paper on the 'S.M.A.R.T. Way to Write Management's Goals and Objectives',[23] which appears to be the first time the system made it into public awareness.

Since then, the SMART method has been widely used and promoted as a useful tool with which to construct goals. The SMART method addresses 5 of the most critical components which need to be considered when formulating clear articulate goals.

It is important to note that the SMART system does not impose a radical insistence that all 5 criteria must be written down and pursued. Rather, the SMART goal acronym provides you with a framework to help guide your thinking as you progress through defining and clarifying your goals.

For instance, not every goal worth achieving is measurable. However, measurement is still a quality which should be considered in every goal, even if you later decide it does not require measurement.

I realise that there are other methods (Acronyms) out there which offer a framework for effective goal setting. Personally, I don't think it is necessary to get hung up on which method is better or worse. At the end of the day, the acronym you use to formulate your goals is less important compared to how you actively pursue your goals. In the end, your success will come down to what you do. Little will depend on which framework you used to write out your goals. As the saying goes, 'Talk is cheap; action speaks much louder than words'. So, let your actions ring loud and clear, and success shall be yours.

In the next section we will consider each letter individually, and what quality each represents.

S - Be Specific

When you set a goal, it is important to be as specific as possible. For example, saying, "I want to get rich", "I want to lose weight", or "I want to go on holiday" is vague, and not likely to be achieved.

The problem with these goals relates to their clarity. Exactly what does it mean to be rich, lose weight or go on holiday? The first step to defining goals is to state them as clearly as possible, so that in your mind's eye you can visually see the outcome.

For instance, can you visualise what possessions you have around you when you are rich? Can you see what car you have parked in the drive way? Can you see the house you are living in, and how much money you have in the bank?

Likewise, you can visualise what your body looks like, and what clothes you are wearing. You might also notice where you are on holiday, what type of accommodation you are staying in, and what activities you are enjoying.

The more detail you can provide, the more likely you will attain your goals. As Brian Tracy said, "People with clear, written goals, accomplish far more in a shorter period of time than people without them could ever imagine." Hence your goals should be clear and unambiguous.

M - Measurable

You should always try and make your goals measurable, so that you can tell when you have achieved them. The world is filled with everyday situations where you need to measure some quantity to achieve your desired result, so this is a skill most of us have already acquired.

For example, when I make gravy, I have to measure 1 cup of water into the jug, before putting in 1 or 2 table spoons of gravy powder. When I fill up my car, I key into the pump the dollar amount which I intend to spend on fuel. The pump then fills the tank to that amount.

You can use the same type of thinking when you set your goals. By including some means to measure your progress, you will be better positioned to know when you have reached your destination.

For example, I might have a goal, 'I want to improve the relationship I have with my teenage children.' The problem with this goal is how to measure progress. How will I know that I am improving my relationship with my children?

One way I can measure this goal is to add a 'progress scale' of some sort to my goal. For instance, I can use a scale from 1 (poor) to 10 (excellent) when I assess my progress on my goal on a daily, weekly or monthly basis. Using this measurement, I can improve the formulation of my goal by saying, 'I want to improve the relationship I have with my teenage children, by achieving a score of 8 or more on my scale by the end of the month.'

A - Achievable

A very good way of self-sabotaging your goals is to make them unachievable. If you set your goals so high that you have little or no chance of achieving them, then you won't even begin to work on them. Your goals will be dead in the water before they even have a chance of success.

For example, if you are currently a part-time assistant manager, and you set a goal of becoming the CEO of a fortune 500 company in less than a year, you may be disappointed. This goal may be too unrealistic to attain. It is good to dream big, and to have audacious goals, but give yourself some room to manoeuvre.

A better approach is to set goals which have incremental steps. For instance, to become a CEO usually entails a long climb up the corporate ladder, gradually achieving one rung at a time. Sometimes you might jump rungs, but usually you don't.

In this instance, it might be better to establish your initial goal as, 'I will become the departmental manager by the end of the year and the divisional manager in two years.' After you have achieved these incremental steps, you might be in a better position to set your sights on becoming CEO.

Another example might be to set a goal to run a marathon in 12 months' time. You could establish your initial goal as, 'I will run one 10 km race in 3 months, one 16 km race in 5 months and two 21 km races in 8 and 10 months' time.' By the time the marathon comes around, you will have achieved several incremental steps, making it much easier and likely that you will achieve your bigger goal of running a marathon, and completing it in a good time.

The point is that it is perfectly fine to think big, but give yourself some room to grow. Start by setting smaller incremental steps which eventually add up to produce the big reward at the end.

A - Action Oriented

A defining attribute of successful people is that they are action orientated. They have come to understand that a desire, wish or want will never materialise into reality, until it has been turned into an actionable goal.

All goals are actionable. You should always consider what kind of action you need to take to achieve your goal, and write your goal in a way that reflects this action.

For example, you might have a goal to learn a new language. Firstly, you should ask yourself what you need to do to make it actionable.

For example, you may need to decide what language you want to learn; be it Spanish, Italian or German. Then you need to consider how you will go about learning it; for instance, you could enrol in a college course, study it by distance learning, or purchase an online course. Also, you should consider how much study time you will be able to allocate to the course each day, and how you will afford to pay for it.

All these considerations will help you define a very specific goal, which you have a far greater chance of achieving. In the end, your final goal might be, 'I will study Russian through an online course for at least two hours per week and pay for it using my savings.'

R - Relevant

How do you know if your goal is relevant?

Firstly, you need to know what your most important values are.

Secondly, you need to define what you want out of life. Once you know this, you will have a better sense of what it is you want to do, be, and own. This knowledge will make goal setting much easier for you, because a relevant goal is one which moves you towards the things you truly desire.

According to www.mars-one.com, NASA has a goal to put people on Mars in the near future. The proposed date is 2024, and NASA has started accepting applications from people all around the world who are willing to undertake this dangerous, yet exciting mission.

In the first call over 200,000 people applied. It's a big deal if you get chosen because according to the website, in 1000 years, everyone on Earth will still remember that you were one of the first humans to set foot on Mars. If you want to etch your name into the history books, you will need to be on that mission.

However, the trip is fraught with many dangers, and with current technology, people who land on Mars, (assuming they make it there in the first place) may never leave the red planet ever again. They may be stuck there for the rest of their lives. This seems to be the case currently, as technology is not capable of getting people back into space once they land on the planet. So do you think you are going to be one of the few people in history to set foot on Mars?

The answer to this question depends on how relevant this goal is to you. Is this goal consistent with your values and desires? If you value family and close relationships, going to Mars may not be a relevant goal, as you will have to leave all your loved ones behind. Being away from your loved ones, which most likely will be forever, may not be consistent with what you hold important in life. Becoming famous, and having your name etched in the history books may be less important to you, than living out your days with your loved ones, and watching your kids grow up.

However, if you value exploring, and being the first to set your feet on distant worlds, then the goal of living out your days on Mars will be very relevant.

For your goals to have the biggest chance of achievement, they should be relevant, and align with your values, beliefs and desires.

R – Realistic

Another important consideration, under the R part of the acronym, is whether your goal is realistic.

To address this issue, you should ask yourself if you have a realistic chance of achieving it.

For instance, is your goal within your physical and mental capabilities? Personally, I believe that in most cases, there is not much you cannot achieve, because as long as you can believe it, you can achieve it.

Naturally, there are some goals which are predisposed to certain physical qualities. Some sports, like Basketball, seem to favour very tall individuals. But, for the most part, most sports do not appear to favour any particular physical dimension.

The same is true of intelligence. Intelligence has been shown to be a poor predictor of success.[36] It is true that intelligence goes a long way to aiding success, but it is not a condition of success. Determination and persistence have proven to be better predictors of success.[26] There are many genius-level individuals out there who have failed miserably at pursuing goals due to their lack of persistence.

For the most part, goals which have already been accomplished by others should be realistic to be achieved by you too.

Whether the goal is realistic for you, or not, is an entirely different question. For example, going back to our Mars example above, it may not be realistic to apply to be on the first flight out if you are very old, terminally ill, or will be in primary school when the space shuttle lifts off from Cape Canaveral.

T – Time Frame

Finally, we get to the last letter in the SMART acronym. All goals should have a time frame; an end date by which they should be completed.

Setting goals like, 'We need to have a meeting next month' or 'I need to do some planning' are vague, and unlikely to get done. Good goal formulation includes a specific time frame with tight deadlines.

When you consider deadlines, remember the effects of Parkinson's Law; work will expand to fill the time you have available for it. If you give your project 6 months to complete, it will most likely take 6 months, even if you could do it in 6 weeks. The work demands will simply fill the time allocated to it. However, this does not mean that every project can be completed faster than your estimate. There are many instances when projects take much longer, and time frames have to be extended (see the planning fallacy in Chapter 11).

Nevertheless, good goal setting practice keeps time frames tight, so that you will push yourself to achieve more in less time. At the same time, you need to remain flexible enough to renegotiate time frames, if your estimates or projections are inaccurate. The aim, at the end of the day, is to work less by becoming more efficient and effective with the time you have available. An improvement on your goal is; 'We will have a 30 minute standing meeting at 2 pm next Tuesday.'

GOAL SETTING GUIDELINES

In the next section we consider some of the guidelines you should follow when formulating good goals.

1. Set both long, and short-term goals

You should always have a list of long term and short term goals.

Long term goals are more like big picture goals, while short term goals are more of the day to day variety.

You need to achieve the short term goals to reach the long term ones. Goal setting is a process of setting and achieving several short term goals, on the way to achieving your bigger long term goals.

Short term goals have many benefits, which include:

- They give you a very specific focal point to focus your attention on.

- They are easily achieved in the short term.

- They provide you with a type of scaffolding, to help you climb higher, and higher, on your journey up the ladder.

- They help you gain confidence in yourself, and in your ability to achieve your dreams.

- They foster greater success, as initial success breeds more success.

How long term goals benefit you:

- They provide you with a big picture of what you want.

- They allow you to plot your course towards your destination. It is easier to notice the smaller steps you need to take, when you have an idea of where you are heading.

- They help you take stock of what you will need to achieve your goal, such as, the skills and knowledge you will need to gain or what physical resources you will need to acquire.

2. Set yourself challenging goals

Research shows that goals must be challenging to be effective.

One of the problems with goal setting, and why people fail to achieve anything significant, is because they only set easily achievable goals, which are goals you can practically achieve in your sleep.

People are goal setting machines. Every day we get up and achieve one goal after another. For example, goals like getting ready to go out by a certain time, dropping kids off at school before the bell rings, getting to work before 9 a.m. or buying the ingredients for the evening meal, are the norm for most people.

Right now, as I write this section, I have to prepare to take my oldest daughter to a boxing class which starts at 5h30 in town. Tomorrow, I have a goal of dropping the same daughter off at her netball match by 11h30, and taking her younger sister to visit the art gallery at 1pm.

Goals like these are common, everyday goals, which are easy to achieve and do not stretch us much at all. For goals to really have any significant and meaningful effect on us, they need to be challenging, and push us to new heights.

To achieve them you might need to learn new skills, develop your mind and body, push yourself beyond what you have ever done before, and break out of your comfort zone. As Robin Sharma said, "successful people do not spend their lives doing what comes easy and comfortable."

3. Identify goal attainment strategies

To achieve your goals, you will need to investigate new strategies and methods to help you achieve them. This requires learning, trial and error, and even courage to step out into the unknown.

Each goal you attempt will require a different type of strategy. There is no one shoe to fit all goals. You may have to take a course, read a book, watch a training video, or consult an expert to learn new skills to help you achieve your goals.

One of my strategies is to search YouTube for how to videos on all sorts of subjects. For instance, I often use YouTube to find out how to use software, or how to set up a piece of computer or printer hardware. Rather than use trial and error, I use a short cut method of learning from someone else that has already done it.

4. Set priorities

Some goals are clearly more important than others. Some goals are so important that when you achieve them, their effect will resolve many of the other goals you have. The realisation of some goals will make a huge difference to your life and situation.

Some goals may also appear contradictory; you may hold one goal which appears to contradict another. For example, imagine you have one goal which is to spend less time training (if you're a marathon runner), but another goal to be the best marathon runner in the world. Marathons are long distance runs which require a large amount of training time.

According to Anders Ericson, it takes 10,000 hours to become a world renowned performer in any field.[30] This means you will need to put in large amounts of time to be great at whatever it is you decide to do. Rough estimates suggest 10 years of consistent practice.[36]

On the surface of it, these two goals appear to contradict each other; how can you train less, and still be the best? You can resolve this conflict by becoming more efficient and getting more out of your practice time. You could consult the best coaches in the world, and discover practice methods you can use in your training that allow you to double your output, in half the time. In the end, you might achieve both goals, which on the surface appear contradictory at first.

There will be times when you will have to prioritise certain goals over others. Confucius said, "The person who chases two rabbit's catches neither", which suggests you should prioritise which rabbit you want to catch, and pursue that one first.

5. Understand the difference between outcome, performance and process goals

The most common types of goals are outcome goals, which depend on elements you have no control over.

For example, you might have an outcome goal to win the Boston Marathon. However, this outcome goal lacks control, as you have no way to control aspects of the event, or the other contestants in the race. Anything can happen on the day, which could disrupt, or destroy your goal. As a result, these goals produce more anxiety and worry.

Performance goals, on the other hand, relate to particular aspects of your performance, like how fast you can run 1km, or your best time over a 21km flat run. Performance goals are specific to you, and do not depend on outside factors beyond your control.

Process goals focus on the actual techniques you use when running, like your running style, body position, breathing technique, and other aspects specific to running long distances.

You will need to establish all three goal types to achieve your dreams.

Your outcome goal might be to win the Boston Marathon, but your performance goal might be to run 10 x 42km training runs in certain time frames. Your process goals are to develop a smooth running style which is upright, with little sideways swaying.

6. Goals stated in the positive are far better than goals stated in the negative.

Which goal do you think is better?

'I don't want to fail my chemistry exam next Monday at 9 am', OR, 'I will pass my chemistry exam next Monday at 9 am, and achieve at least 90% by studying a chapter every day from today until Sunday'

The first goal is counterproductive, as it highlights failure, and the difficulty of passing Chemistry. This is inconsistent with what you want, which is to pass your exam with 90% or more. The negatively framed goal does not tell you what to do.

The alternative version is stated in a positive tone, and the emphasis is on what you want to achieve, rather than what you don't want. It also tells you how you will do it. Stating goals in the positive is a far better way of formulating your goals.

HOW TO IMPLEMENT SMART GOALS

Now that we have covered the SMART goal setting method, it is time to implement the process. Let's go back to your Master List from Chapter 3, and decide which 10 items on that list are the most important to you (The number 10 is purely arbitrary at this stage).

Write a goal for each of the 10 items from your list in the boxes below. Once you have formulated a goal, assess it with the Quality check box. Most importantly, you want to ensure your goals are SMART and that they are consistent with your values (See your list of values in Chapter 2). Assessing each goal one at a time, put a tick in the Quality Check box if the goal is SMART, and is consistent with your values.

Exercise 1: Setting 10 SMART Goals

No	Goal	Quality Check
1		
2		
3		
4		
5		
6		
7		
8		
9		
10		

Goal Prioritisation Exercise

In this exercise, you will prioritise your list of SMART goals from Exercise 1. Copy your goals into the boxes below. After you have copied all 10 goals, please follow the goal prioritisation strategy in the next section.

Exercise 2: Prioritising 10 SMART goals

No	Goal	Priority

Goal Prioritisation Strategy

Now that you have your top 10 goals copied into the table, it is time to prioritise them. Starting at goal 1, compare this goal to goal 2, and decide which of these two goals is the most important. If goal 1 is more important, then put goal 2 aside for the moment and compare goal 1 to goal 3 on your list. Now decide which is more important, goal 1 or 3,. If it is still goal 1, continue down to the next goal (e.g. 4), following the same process as before. Do this with each goal, and assuming you find no goal more important than goal 1, you will reach the end of the list. If no other goal is more important than goal 1, then write a 1 in the priority box corresponding to goal 1.

If however, you discover another goal which is more important than goal 1, for example goal 6, then put goal 1 aside for the moment, and continue the process down the list with goal 6. So in this case compare goal 6 to goal 7 and decide which is more important. You don't have to compare goal 6 to the goals above it on the list, because you already know it's more important than those goals.

Following this process you will uncover your No 1 goal and the priority of all the other goals on your list. You should continue with the same process to discover your No 2, 3 etc. goals until you have examined all 10.

At the end of this exercise, you should have the goal which will make the biggest difference in your life right now, if you were able to achieve it at this very moment. It should be the goal which will give you the greatest reward. If the goal you have listed as your No 1 Goal does not appear to have much of an impact on your life, and doesn't make much of an effect on resolving your many other goals, then one of the following issues may exist:

1. **This goal is not your No 1 Goal.** You may need to revisit the previous exercises you used to define what you

want out of life, and set more goals to compare with (see Chapter 2). Possibly, you have not uncovered your most important goal yet. Take your time as you progress through the exercises, think deeply about what you want to be, do, and have in life. Use blue sky thinking, and imagine that you can achieve anything, that you have no limits, and nothing is holding you back. Let your mind soar, and your imagination take you to new destinations.

2. **The No 1 Goal you have determined is not really your goal.** It might be what someone else wants for you. In this exercise you need to set goals which are important to you! You cannot truly succeed in life, unless you fully commit to your objectives. Once again, revisit the previous exercises and determine what *you* want in life (not what someone else wants for you).

3. **During the process of comparison you have over-rated the importance of a particular goal.** Go back to exercise 2, and compare your goals again with one another. The problem with this exercise is that other people's voices will come into the picture as you rate your goals. Many times we will push other people's goals ahead of our own, due to social conditioning, fear, or any number of psychological issues at play in our minds and lives. We want to please, which at times results in us becoming swayed by other people's whims. Hence, their goals seem to take precedence over ours, and our needs get pushed aside. You may need to keep this in mind while you prioritise your goals.

Your Most Important Focus

Your No 1 Goal will represent your most important focus, and the one thing you should fixate your energy and attention on above all other things. To be successful in achieving your desires, and reaching your most important goals, you will have to spend the majority of your productive time pursuing your No 1 Goal.

The Pareto Principal

You may have heard the story of Italian born Vilfredo Pareto (1848), who once (around 1897) noticed that 20 % of the pea plants in his vegetable garden generated 80% of the total healthy pea pods.

Pareto decided to look for other types of uneven distributions, and found many. He discovered that 20% of the Italian population owned 80% of the land. He found the same effect reoccurring in industry, where he noticed that 80% of production was produced by 20% of the companies.

Pareto was a quality control pioneer, and using his keen eye for unequal distributions, noticed that a handful of flaws would produce the majority of defects. He went on to write a mathematical income distribution model, which today is commonly known as Pareto's Principle, the principle of least effort (80/20 rule).

What Pareto discovered so many years ago is a real phenomenon, just like the law of gravity. Some believe it is possibly one of the greatest productivity truths ever discovered.[50]

According to Pareto, the majority is governed by the minority. Extraordinary results are disproportionately created by the fewest actions, for example:

20% of your ideas will account for 80% of your results

20% of salespeople account for 80% of the sales

20% of customers account for 80% of the business

20% of software bugs account for 80% of computer crashes

20% of patients account for 80% of health care costs

20% of your investments account for 80% of your returns

20% of your clothes are worn 80% of the time

20% of criminals account for 80% of the crime

20% motorists account for 80% of the accidents

20% of your carpet gets 80% of the wear

20% of the streets get 80% of the traffic

20% beer drinkers drink 80% of the beer

20% of married people account for 80% of the divorces

20% of the foods you eat will account for 80% of your weight gain

20% of your goals will produce 80% of your rewards

If anything, the 80/20 rule demonstrates the importance of focusing on less, to achieve more. It highlights the importance of discovering your No 1 Goal, and then pursuing this with purpose and persistence.

Following the 80/20 rule, we know that 20% of your goals from exercise 2 will account for 80% of your success, or rewards. In the table below, write down your top 2 goals from your list (20% of 10 goals equals just 2 goals). These two goals, assuming you have defined what you want and prioritised your top 10 goals correctly, should provide you with your biggest rewards.

Exercise 3: Your Top 2 Goals

No	Goal
1	
2	

A Personal Example

This goal setting and comparison exercise is really effective in helping you discover your most important priorities in life, and finding creative ways to pursue them. For example, after completing this exercise, one of the top goals I decided on was to spend more time with my family, particularly my kids.

I decided I would seek out opportunities to spend quality 1 on 1 time with each child, and my wife, once a month. I decided to set aside time every month to do something special with each of them. At the time, I was working full-time on my PhD at Otago University, and we were living on a bare bones income from my scholarship.

Nonetheless, I had decided that this goal was important to me, and there was no better time to build good memories with my family than right then. I set aside a small budget to do something special with each person once per month.

It didn't take long before we all started looking forward to our day out together, and sometimes we would start discussing what we were going to do days, or weeks, in advance.

It has been well over a year now since I implemented this strategy, and I still maintain this as one of my top 10 goals.

To me, it's like a perpetual rotating goal, which I plan on maintaining for as long as possible. There is no better time than right now to build good memories with your most precious and important people in your life. Although this goal was not in my top 2 goals, it is one of my best goals.

The emergence of your best goals

The first time I did the goal setting exercise above, I had many more goals than 10. As time passed, I found that I could quickly knock several goals off my list, because they were either easily achieved, or they were not worth pursuing. Eventually after a few weeks my most important goals started to emerge.

A few of those goals are still current, and I still keep working on them as they represent some of my most important goals. These goals are the ones which will make the biggest difference in my life, once achieved. Gary Keller, author of *The One Thing: The surprisingly truth behind extraordinary results,*[48] describes these goals as your 'One Thing'. Keller gives the example of the domino effect, to illustrate the power of focusing on your 'One Thing.'

In 1983, physicist Lorne Whitehead, from the University of British Columbia, demonstrated the true power of the domino effect. As showcased by professor Stephen Morris from the University of Toronto, dominoes can knock down things about 1.5 times their size.

Starting from a domino just five inches tall, says Morris, it would take just 29 progressively larger dominoes to wipe out the Empire State Building – that's right, just 29 dominoes. The Empire State Building has 102 floors and has a height of 443 meters to the tip. You just need 29 dominoes, with each successive domino being just 1.5 times the size of the previous domino to topple it.

In 2001, a physicist from the San Francisco Exploratorium reproduced the domino experiment, by creating 8 dominos from plywood. The first domino was a tiny 2 inches tall, the last 3 feet. The first domino fell over with a gentle tick, but this ended in a large bang by the 8th.

This is the effect of focusing on your No 1 Goal. By putting all your energy, focus, and effort into just one primary goal, you can light a fire which will literally light up the world.

The importance of finding your No 1 Goal is probably the single most significant factor in determining whether you will attain massive success, or just slip back into mediocrity. The importance of this point can't be emphasised enough.

Embrace small steps

Small steps are probably the most important goals you can set. Each small step adds up to produce a huge outcome. When you look back, all those small steps will have helped you climb higher, and higher, towards your ultimate goal. Think of it like this little story by Jacob August Riis (May 3, 1849 – May 26, 1914), "When nothing seems to help, I go and look at a stonecutter hammering away at his rock perhaps a hundred times without as much as a crack showing in it. Yet at the hundred and first blow it will split in two, and I know it was not that blow that did it, but all that had gone before."

For the stone cutter, each strike at the rock made a small measurable, though physically unnoticeable, difference. The effects of his efforts would have been scarcely visible, yet he trusted the process, and kept hammering away. Eventually, all of his efforts came together in one single moment to produce the success he was working towards – and the rock split.

Another excellent example of how small daily changes can radically transform your life, is found in Darren Hardy's book, *The Compound Effect*.[39] Hardy said, "If you were given a choice between taking $3 million in cash this very instant and a single penny that doubles in value every day for 31 days, which would you choose?" Most people would jump at the 3 million given the chance, but the wise individual will choose the single penny, because after 31 days the compound effect will have increased that single penny to $10,737,418.24.

YOUR MISSION STATEMENT

"To leave a positive legacy"

David Barton

A mission statement simply describes what it is you do, what your purpose is, and why you exist. Now that you have set your primary goal/s, and established your focus, you can set your mission statement for yourself and/or your business. Consider the following questions as you define your personal mission statement:

Exercise 4: Your Personal Mission Statement

1. What do I exist to do?

2. Who do I work for?

3. How do I do what I do?

The best way to write up a mission statement is to keep it simple, short and straight to the point. It does not need to look too far ahead - 3 years max. You, and everyone else who works with you, should be able to articulate your mission statement at the drop of a hat.

Mission statements should be inspiring, clear, and easy to remember: Don't underestimate this factor. If they are difficult to remember, they won't be of much use to you, or your organisation.

Here are a few mission statements that I believe fit the bill very nicely. They are the mission statements from 5 non-profit companies:

1. **TED**: Spread Ideas.

2. **Smithsonian**: Understanding the natural world and our place in it.

3. **The Humane Society**: Celebrating Animals, Confronting Cruelty.

4. **Wounded Warrior Project**: To honour and empower wounded warriors.

5. **Best Friends Animal Society**: To bring about a time when there are no more homeless pets.

As you can see, these mission statements are incredibly short, succinct and to the point, and yet remarkably impactful.

Your mission statement should reflect what it is you do

It will be easy for people working at TED to remember their mission statement: "spreading ideas". If you walk around that organisation, and ask any person who works there, "what is your mission statement?", in all likelihood they will easily know what it is. Ted talks spread ideas. They do what their mission statement says they do. They have world renowned speakers giving talks on all sorts of interesting and useful topics. Their mission statement is representative of what they do.

Your mission statement should represent your core values

You should also be able to live your mission statement. How easy will it be to live The Humane Society's mission to celebrate animals and confront cruelty? I imagine that the people who work for this organisation are doing exactly that. They confront cruelty daily, head on, and do everything in their power to protect animal rights. For them, animals are to be celebrated and not abused. This is a statement you can live. This speaks about their core values.

Your mission statement should reflect positivity and inspiration

Mission statements should be inspiring, and capture a positive sense of hopefulness. One of Coca Cola's mission statements is 'To refresh the world'. You can see how Coke lives out this mission in their advertising. Usually, it is filled with people celebrating by opening a cold coke on a hot or tiring day, and feeling refreshed as a result.

Now it's your turn to create your own mission statement.

My Mission Statement

_____

_____

_____

_____

_____

_____

KEY POINTS TO REMEMBER

- SMART goals have been around for quite some time. The acronym is useful for thinking through the various components which go into establishing good goals.

- SMART stands for specific, measurable, achievable, actionable, realistic, relevant and time frame.

- SMART goals really are smart, because once you have considered each component of the goal you will be able to take a more logical and relational perspective of the goal.

- Not only should you consider the individual items in the SMART acronym, you should also follow certain guidelines when establishing your goals.

- One of the most important guidelines is to set difficult to reach, but not impossible, goals. These goals will stretch you and help you grow.

- Each person will have many goals. We all have goals for different parts of our lives. However, there is probably 1 or 2 goals in our lives which will produce the greatest reward for us. If you achieve this 1 goal you will resolve many other goals at the same time.

- Your most important goal has far reaching effects. Its realisation will impact several areas of your life. It is the goal you should spend most of your time, effort and resources pursuing.

- You should set your own mission statement. Most of the best companies in the word have a mission statement which guides their actions.

- Mission statements should be easy to remember and easy to live.

CHAPTER 5

Planning Your Goals For Success

*"Setting a goal is not the main thing. It is
deciding how you will go about achieving it
and staying with that plan."*

Tom Landry

Now that you have set your top 10 goals, and more importantly, uncovered your No 1 Goal, you can begin the process of planning. As Tom Landry correctly states, goal setting is not the main event. Just setting your goal is not enough; achieving your goal will require a plan, and the systematic and deliberate activation of that plan.

In this Chapter you will learn a basic planning process to guide you through the most critical aspects of planning your SMART goals.

You will examine plans, strategies and tactics employed by two teams of explorers who raced to be the first to reach the South Pole in 1911. Their story highlights several critical aspects of planning and goal setting, which we can use to guide and implement our own plans.

SUCCESSFUL GOALS PLANNING

Recently I read the riveting account of two teams of explorers who attempted to reach the South Pole in 1911.[69] It was during the "Heroic Age of Antarctic Exploration," and the South Pole was one of the last unexplored places on earth.

The first team was led by Robert Falcon Scott, who hoped to claim the bottom of the world for England; while the second team was guided by Norwegian, Ronald Amundsen, who intended to claim to the title in honour of his countrymen and King.

Compared to today, in 1910 it was much tougher to reach the Antarctic by ship, never mind travel to the South Pole on foot. Nevertheless, both parties miraculously reached the South Pole; one group had a relatively smooth trip, while the other group died on their way back to base camp.

There is much we can learn from this true story, not just about persistence and grit, but also about goal setting, planning and preparation.

The Goal: Get To The South Pole First

Both Scott and Amundsen had the same goal; to reach the South Pole first. However, their planning and preparation was quite different. Each one approached his goal in a different manner, and each one experienced different results.

For one, Amundsen and his team reached the South Pole first, and all returned to their base camp alive. Their entire trip was relatively smooth, fast and straightforward. Their strategy was reminiscent of a modern day Navy Seal mission to a foreign country. They got in, completed their mission, and got out as soon as possible.

On the other hand, Scott and his team struggled the entire way, having faced one difficulty after another. The trip was long, difficult, and exhausting. In the end they all died, having faced starvation, exhaustion, and exposure on their 700 mile return trip.

A good lesson to take from their account is that there are times when reaching for your dreams will cost you your life.

At times you will fail at achieving your goal and you might have to face similarly huge disappointments, as Scott did when arriving at 90° south, only to find Amundsen's flags already flapping in the wind.

It was not this single factor alone which precipitated his teams demise; it was a combination of several other miscalculations and planning errors, which eventually caused their deaths.

Scott and Amundsen were both good leaders; each man had his strengths and weaknesses, and each man utilised a different strategy to achieve his goals.

What is interesting about this story is that both parties were in the same geographical location, at the same time. Both parties were facing similar conditions and challenges. Yet, one prevailed and the other succumbed to the elements. Their specific outcomes, to a large degree, resulted from the quality of their planning and preparation.

How good is your planning and preparation?

Author and speaker, Brian Tracy, is famous for claiming, "Every minute you spend in planning saves you 10 minutes in execution; this gives you a 1,000% return on energy!" What this means is planning has the potential to multiply your efforts in several important ways, which may include:

1. **Time**. Planning has the benefit of saving you time in execution. For instance, the team Scott chose to travel with him to the South Pole was scaled back to just 5, including himself. All 5 men were dead 150 days after departing from their base camp. In comparison, Amundsen and his 4 other crew members all got to the South Pole and back to their base camp in just 99 days. They reached the South Pole 34 days

ahead of Scott. A good plan has the power to save you precious time in execution.

2. **Speed**. Planning has the benefit of improving your speed of delivery. Amundsen's dog drawn sleds could travel at twice the speed of Scott's man hauling teams. Scott's expedition was also far more complex than Amundsen's, which drastically effected his speed of delivery. Scott initially started out with 16 men, 23 dogs, 10 ponies, 13 sledges, and 2 motor sledges. Each of these forms of transport could make progress at different speeds, which meant that for them all to arrive at the same time at the next camp, they had to leave at different times in the morning.

3. **Energy**. Planning has the benefit of reducing your energy expenditure. Scott's team required much more energy to man-haul their sleds ¾ of the trip, while Amundsen and his team rode there and back on dog drawn sleds. Scott's men needed to consume more food as a result, but due to poor planning, the food rations for the day barely covered the men's energy demands.

4. **Risk Reduction**. Planning has the benefit of reducing your risk and exposure to danger. Every noteworthy and challenging goal you attempt will have a certain amount of risk and danger associated with it. You can reduce your risk exposure through good planning, preparation, and persistence. To succeed at your objective, you will need to try and weigh the balance more in your favour by minimising the risk as much as possible. Amundsen's 'Navy Seal' approach to achieving his goal was a good example of this. He and his team arrived in hostile territory and got in and out, completing their mission as fast as possible. In comparison, Scott and his team made a slow and laborious trek though hostile terrain, which drastically increased their exposure to risk, and eventually ended in their demise.

GOOD PLANS TAKE TIME

Amundsen spent well over a year planning his goal to reach the South Pole, and his thoroughness paid dividends. What we can learn from his example may provide us with useful insights on how we too can reach our highest goals.

Modern Life Is A Busy Life

There is always something else needing done. Who has time to sit down and make a clear, articulate plan? Amundsen did. For instance, he spent a whole year planning where to deposit supplies along his route. His depots were laid out with strict regularity, at each line of latitude, and stocked with ten times more food than Scott had deposited.

Scott and his men died partly from starvation, but Amundsen and his men gained weight on the return trip, because their depots had so much excess food.

When Scott started to lay down the plans for his expedition, he based much of his planning on what Ernest Shackleton had done during his attempt at reaching the South Pole in 1907. Shackleton had come within 112 miles of the South Pole before turning back, himself being close to starvation. Basing your plans on what others have done is not always the best strategy. Sometimes you need to forge your own path and travel your own course.

Forge Your Own Path

Scott not only based his camp at the same location as Shackleton, but he also followed the same route as Shackleton had taken. Scott essentially repeated the same process as Shackleton had, but this time he hoped for a different outcome.

Scott only devised his depot-laying plan once he had arrived at McMurdo Sound. He gave his men 1 week to organise the supplies, and calculate how much food to leave at each depot. The end result was that they only had enough food to scrape by. Scott's team needed far more energy than Amundsen, as they were man hauling ¾ of the way, while Amundsen was travelling by dog drawn sled. The rations allocated to each man in Scott's group were a meagre 4,500 calories a day, but they needed at least 7,000 calories for a normal day, and up to 11,000 when pulling uphill. This lack of food weakened and demoralised the men in Scott's team.

Good Planning Helps You To Notice Alternative Strategies

Amundsen, on the other hand, made his base camp at an entirely different location, called the Bay of Whales. This site had the advantage of being a good 60 miles closer to the South Pole; reducing the round trip by 120 miles. However, no previous explorer had camped at this location before as it was on the edge of the Great Ice Barrier, and some feared it would fracture and float away.

Amundsen, however, had meticulously studied previous records, and discovered the ice had remained unchanged for decades, thereby suggesting it was stable and worth the risk. From here, Amundsen pioneered a new route inland, which no other explorer had ever taken. He plotted the straightest route possible to the South Pole, in uncharted territory. It was riskier, but then risk is a factor in any major pursuit, and Amundsen was willing to accept this.

A critical aspect of goal setting, and undoubtedly one of the central themes of this book, is that you should always pursue your No 1 Goal first and foremost, above all other goals. Research shows that willpower is reduced when you have to make a decision based on too many choices.[45] You will experience more mental fatigue by the extra demands placed on your limited cognitive capacities. In the end this weakens your resolve and taxes your resources more than if you simply focused on one single pursuit at a time.

Be clear about your goals, as your life could depend on it!

One of the big differences between Amundsen and Scott, was that Amundsen had just one single goal in mind: to be the first to reach the South Pole. Scott, on the other hand, had dual objectives. Firstly, it was to get to the South Pole first, and secondly, to gather scientific information about the Antarctic. Scott's purposes were divided.

It may have been these dual focuses which eventually cost Scott and his men their lives. At one point along their return leg, Scott and his men had just 5 days of food left, and they were about five days walk from their next food supply depot. They were already exhausted and struggling.

Because the weather had improved, they made a short detour to collect rock samples. These rock samples added extra weight to their sleds which consequently slowed them down further and required more energy to pull. The little detour added 7-8 extra miles in the opposite direction, which needed to be recovered.

Keep in mind, that when they eventually found Scott and the other 2 remaining men dead in their tents, they were a mere 12 miles from 1 Ton Depot, where they would have found plenty of food and fuel which could have saved their lives.

Dual purpose goals have the power to divide and defeat you

This is an example of what dual purpose goals can do. They divide your attention and resources, and sometimes you end up losing everything as a result.

Scott, could have easily come back to conduct these scientific inquiries later on, after he had returned to base and recovered, but he chose not to. Dual purpose goals create a psychological weight which needs to be resolved. One way to resolve it is to put some time and effort into the goal, but this comes at a cost to your other, more important goals.

Amundsen was clear on his primary purpose, and planned to do nothing else but focus on this one thing. Amundsen demonstrates this clarity of purpose in even small tasks, like taking fewer photographs; Scott's team took a whopping 2,000 photographs and Amundsen took only 10 (and these only once they'd reached the South Pole).

Regarding Amundsen's approach to achieving his No 1 Goal, he wrote, "Our plan is one, one and again one alone–to reach the pole. For that goal, I have decided to throw everything else aside. We shall do what we can without colliding with this plan. If we were to have a night watch, we would have a light burning the whole time. In one room, as we have, this would be worrying for most of us, and make us weak. What concerns me is that we all live properly in all respects during the winter. Sleep and eat well, so that we have full strength and are in good spirits when spring arrives to fight towards the goal which we must attain at any cost."

Amundsen's plan was single minded and straight forward; his goal was clear and simple. He planned to race to the South Pole and be the first one to get there. Everything Amundsen did in his preparation and execution of his plan resounded with this clear intent. The end result was that he and his team survived to tell the story.

So what is your No 1 Goal? In Chapter 4, you did an exercise to formulate your most important goals and priorities. The process helped you prioritise your most important goals. Please write your No 1 Goal in the space below. If you don't recall it from memory, then please go back and remind yourself now.

My Number 1 Goal

WHY DO YOU WANT TO ACHIEVE THIS GOAL?

To achieve your number one goal, you need to be motivated. The best way to motivate yourself is to have many good reasons why you want the goal in the first place.

Ask Yourself:

Why do I want to achieve this goal so badly?

Why do I want to achieve this particular goal and not another one instead?

What's so special about this particular goal?

These are the types of questions Amundsen and Scott would have been asking themselves. The reasons they had to achieve their No 1 Goal, would have fuelled their resolve and empowered their actions.

Amundsen and Scott were, in part, motivated by the same thing; they wanted to be the first people to set foot on the South Pole, and in so doing immortalise themselves in the history books (you are reading about them now, so it worked).

We are all motivated by different things. So what motivates you? What gets you out of bed in the morning? For example, are you motivated by fame and fortune?

For both Amundsen and Scott there was quite a substantial pay day awaiting them in terms of book royalties, speaking engagements, public appearances, and product endorsements, which usually accompanies those with celebrity status.

They would have been widely admired and highly regarded by their peers, and the public in general. They would have been considered heroes.

Possibly, they would have proved a few things to themselves, regarding their toughness, courage and skills.

For Scott, he may have found reward in the educational advances he and his team would produce through their findings.

Successfully completing their mission to the South Pole would have opened up many more doors to funding avenues for future exploration. Personally, I don't think it would have mattered in the end who got to the South Pole first, the fact they did it in the first place was remarkable. To have survived such a major ordeal was enough of an accomplishment to warrant future support and access to sponsorship, to fund further missions to distant and unexplored places.

As you can see, Amundsen and Scott would have had many good reasons to motivate themselves towards their No 1 Goal. When times were really hard, and the situation looked bleak, they could cling to their motivations to help them press on through the blizzards and storms.

They wanted their goal more than anything. They were willing to die, if it came to that. Now that is serious commitment, and the kind that gets results – big earth shattering results.

Now, considering the lessons Scott and Amundsen have taught us, ask yourself the following questions:

What are my reasons for wanting to achieve my No 1 Goal?

Is it something I am willing to die for?

Is it something I am willing to sink everything I have into?

WHAT STEPS DO YOU NEED TO TAKE TO ACHIEVE YOUR PLAN?

To achieve any major undertaking in life may require hundreds of small steps. Your No 1 Goal is the vision you have for your future; it is the outcome you imagine, the destination you have planned.

It is the incremental steps you take which will eventually get you there. The journey of a thousand miles starts with the very first step, and each step gets you one step closer. Each step you complete represents the next rung in the ladder you need climb to get to the top of your mountain.

When planning a trip to the South Pole, regardless if it's in 1911 or 2016, you will need to have a clear plan, with a multitude of sub-goals.

Both Scott and Amundsen had hundreds of sub-goals, which they needed to complete to get the expedition under way. For one, each man needed a ship, and not just any old ship. They needed one which would not break apart in sea ice. These were also not easy to come by back in their day.

Likewise, they needed a crew; they needed people who could withstand the polar weather, solitary lifestyle and harsh living conditions. They needed transportation, supplies, accommodation, equipment, food, and a raft of other resources.

Each one of these items required special attention. Each one represented a small step in the process of achieving their No 1 Goal.

They also needed to plan their trip to Antarctica; where to make landfall, establish their base camp, what route to take to the South Pole, where to deposit their supplies along the route, on what date to leave for the Pole, what animals to take, which people to take, what clothes to wear, and so on.

One of the key steps both teams needed to take, was laying down their critical supplies along the route. In addition, they also had to make provision to easily locate the depots particularly in a blizzard or thick fog. Amundsen came well prepared for this. He placed a line of ten black flags, spaced a half mile apart, on both sides of his depots. If they came within a few miles of the depots they would run into one of the flags, which had instructions about the direction and distance to the next depot. Amundsen and his men did not miss a single depot on their return trip.

Scott marked his depots with just one flag. On their return trip he missed several depots, as they were too difficult to find. A simple step like laying out flags may seem unimportant at first but in the end could turn out to be critical.

Each step is important, and each step represents important advancements in the achievement of your highest objectives.

So, what steps do you need to take to achieve your No 1 Goal?

WHAT RESOURCES DO YOU NEED TO ACHIEVE YOUR PLAN?

Most goals will need to be resourced. The nature, complexity, and difficulty of your goal will determine the type of resources you will need.

Going to the South Pole will be very resource intensive. You will need particular equipment and transportation. It is a goal which will be quite difficult to achieve. The difficulty of this goal pales in comparison to NASA's goal of placing people on Mars.

Each goal will have its own list of demands and resource requirements, and you need to consider each one if you intend to arrive at your desired destination.

Today, people primarily fly in to the South Pole. Practically nobody plans to walk there. Walking there is ludicrous, because the average summer temperature in Antarctica is −28.2° C (−18° F) and in winter it is −60° C (76° F). Water freezes at 0° C (−32° F), so imagine how cold it is in summer in Antarctica, never mind winter. And the wind is even worse. It can blast through there at incredible speeds, creating some of the worst blizzards on earth.

You will probably agree with me then, that if your only option to reach the South Pole was by foot, then the quicker you got there, and back, the better. The least amount of exposure you had in the below freezing temperatures, the better your chances of survival would be. Back in 1911, going by foot was the only viable method to reach the South Pole. The only real choice was the means by which you could travel across the landscape, with the available options being walking, using animals, or using both animals and walking.

This was also one of the biggest differences between Scott and Amundsen. They each had their own ideas of what forms of transportation was most suitable for their journey.

Scott had four different options in mind. He considered ponies, dogs, motor sledges (primitive snowmobiles), and man-hauling as his best options. Each had their advantages and disadvantages.

Ponies could pull much more weight than humans and dogs, but they needed to feed on vegetation, which Antarctica has none of. Ponies also sweat through their hides, which creates sheets of ice on their bodies and they are heavy animals and easily sink into the snow. This makes moving in Antarctica incredibly difficult for them. Ponies also suffer from snow blindness and need eye protection.

Motor-sledges were very expensive to acquire, were untested in Arctic conditions, but could carry a fair amount of weight, and only required fuel, which took up less space than Pony food. Motor-sledges also didn't sink into the snow, so were a good option if they worked.

Unfortunately, all the ponies had to be put down. They were just not equipped to handle the harsh conditions. They were slow and suffered greatly in the freezing ice and snow. The Motor-sledges were even worse, both broke down not far from the base camp, and this resulted in men having to haul the extra weight the rest of the way on foot.

The dogs performed gamely, but Scott considered them unreliable, and feared they would fall into crevasses which pocketed the terrain. He sent them home after they had completed just ½ the journey to the South Pole.

Men were left to haul the supplies the rest of the way, about 1,000 miles and a climb of 10,000 feet. Progress was slow and exhausting. But Shackleton and other British explorers had used man-hauling as their primary means of polar travel in the past, and it was considered the best—and the most noble–way to go.

Scott wrote, "In my mind no journey ever made with dogs can approach the height of that fine conception which is realised when a party of men go forth to face hardships, dangers, and difficulties with their own unaided efforts...Surely in this case the conquest is more nobly and splendidly won."

Scott's team arrived in Antarctica with 65 men, 19 ponies, 32 dogs, and 3 motor sledges (one didn't make it to shore, it fell through the ice and landed on the bottom of the sea while they were unloading the ship). All these resources, bar men, were disbanded after only ¼ of the journey, leaving the remaining ¾ to be completed through man hauling. Eventually, the final push to the South Pole was completed by just 5 men.

However, Amundsen was more interested in survival than beefing up his manhood. In his mind, there was no glory in dying out in the snow pulling sleds.

Amundsen brought with him 19 men, and around 140 dogs. Amundsen considered man-hauling an activity to be avoided at all costs. He put his full faith in the ability of dogs to get the job done, and they did marvellously.

On a previous mission, he had spent some time among the Netsilik Inuit, learning their ways. He learned about clothing and how to handle dogs. He believed that Inuit dogs were perfectly suited for polar exploration; he also learned that Norwegian Skis were superior to North American snow shoes, and he learned that Greenland dress and modes of living could aid Europeans to prosper and survive in the harshest conditions on Earth. The resource he chose to bring to Antarctica in greater supply was dogs, sleds, skis, Polar clothing, and food fit for polar conditions.

In a sense, his resource list was far simpler than Scott's, and cost much less. This is another benefit of developing clarity about what it is you want to achieve. You only end up needing to acquire the resources you need. Compared to Scott, Amundsen's resource needs provided him the following advantages:

- His resource needs were simpler and his entire approach was easier to accomplish.

- He could move faster, freer and unrestricted by his baggage.

- Implementing his plan was more efficient and smooth.

- He was less exposed to the dangers of the environment.

So what are the most important resources you need to complete your No 1 Goal?

WHAT SKILLS AND KNOWLEDGE WILL YOU NEED TO ACHIEVE YOUR PLAN?

Every major undertaking you will ever attempt will require certain skills and knowledge. You may already have much of what you need to get started, but most likely you will have to gain new skills and more knowledge and information to succeed.

What new knowledge do you need to gain to achieve your goals?

Part of both Scott and Amundsen's preparation for the trip to the South Pole involved gaining as much knowledge about their mission as possible.

From a young age, Amundsen used to attend lectures given by polar explorers, and he tried to learn everything he could about polar exploration from people who had been there. Amundsen gleaned a great deal from Norwegian born Eivind Astrup, who accompanied Peary to Greenland on his 1891-92 expedition.

On some of Amundsen's own explorations of the North, he spent some time with the Inuit and learned much from them about survival and travel in harsh Polar conditions.

Amundsen was Norwegian and had well developed skills on skis. British explorers were far less skilled in this capacity. It is not surprising that skis were an integral part of Amundsen's strategy to reach the pole.

Likewise, Scott had his sources of information. Scott had been to the South Pole before, on a previous Discovery expedition in 1902 from which he gained much experience. He learned from Shackleton's Nimrod expedition in 1907, and based much of his preparations and planning on the conditions Shackleton had reported.

Scott did not count on Antarctica's temperamental weather system. In 1911, the race to the South Pole was accompanied by a particularly harsh winter season, one which only occurs every couple of decades, with powerful blizzards and even more freezing temperatures (as if it wasn't bad enough under normal conditions).

Questions to ask to assess your knowledge and skills:

1. **What sources of information do you have to help you plan your goals?**

2. **What people do you need to contact to help you achieve your goals?**

3. **What expertise do you need to develop to succeed at your goal?**

What Barriers And Obstacles And Challenges Will You Need To Overcome To Achieve Your Plan?

Your goals will often only be gained after you have overcome what can seem like insurmountable challenges.

Difficulties will spring up from the most unlikely places to knock you off track and steer you onto the wrong path.

It is important to make an assessment of potential challenges, as best as possible, to help prepare you for the journey ahead. When troubles come you will be better prepared and ready to handle them.

There are many challenges which await explorers to the South Pole. In this part of the world there is only one sunrise and one sunset a year. The sun rises at the September equinox and stays above the horizon until the March equinox. Then it goes dark until September. This would prove challenging for most people. Our body clocks are not designed to handle situations like this very well. Hence, like pole explorers, you need to be adaptable and flexible to meet your challenges head on.

The South Pole is also incredibly cold. On average Antarctic temperatures are incredibly cold, with the average summer temperature of −28.2° C (−18° F) and winter −60° C (76° F).

This temperature aspect would certainly be a major physical and psychological challenge to most people. Hence, to achieve your No 1 Goal you will need to make a careful and detailed analysis of your challenges, and prepare for them accordingly, just like Amundsen and Scott had to do.

Another challenge facing polar explorers is food supply. Nothing grows in this icy desert waste land. The region has no plants, and at the South Pole there is no life at all. Nothing can survive in such a harsh environment. Polar explorers had to face the prospect of starvation and malnutrition. While they were in camp, they had enough provisions to sustain themselves, but once out in the field, the situation changed drastically.

Because Amundsen had prepared his crew during the winter months for their inland journey, regularly feeding them on almost raw seal meat, he trained their bodies to deal with the problem of scurvy. Seal meat, when it is raw, contains trace amounts of vitamin C, which can ward off symptoms of scurvy.

Scott on the other hand, did not establish a similar system, and his men ate mostly refined foods during their winter wait. In the end, Scott and his companions suffered from the effects of scurvy. This may have contributed to their eventual demise out in the field.

Eating uncooked seal meat is a challenge in itself, which demonstrates how unenjoyable and uncomfortable it can be at times trying to reach your No 1 Goal. It is in those moments, when you are faced with the stark reality of the challenge you need to overcome, that you will discover whether you are willing to do what it takes to ascend the heights of your highest dreams and desires.

These are just some of the many challenges faced by Scott, Amundsen and their crew. But, we all have our own barriers to climb and challenges to face. How we do this in the face of these difficulties will determine if we succeed or fail.

Challenges can present themselves in many different forms:

- Physical Challenges

- Psychological Challenges

- Spiritual Challenges

- Social Challenges
- Family Challenges

In future Chapters, I will address 4 additional challenges which we will all have to face to reach our No 1 Goals. These are perseverance, self-discipline, procrastination and courage.

Now take a moment and reflect on some of the challenges you will have to address on the road to achieving your No 1 Goal.

KEY POINTS TO REMEMBER

- Your goal is just a wish, fantasy or dream, until it is accompanied by a written plan to achieve it.

- Those who fail to plan, plan to fail. 10 minutes of planning can save you 100 minutes in execution.

- Good planning can radically improve your speed of delivery and execution.

- Good planning can reduce your exposure to danger even to the point of saving your life.

- A good plan takes a bird's eye view of the terrain and plots the best course to your target. Good plans contain many steps (sub-goals), which each contribute to the eventual attainment of your objective.

- Good plans take into account your current skills and abilities and makes a reasonable assessment of your knowledge deficiencies.

- Good plans address the necessary resources and materials you will need if you hope to reach your destination.

- A good plan considers the various challenges, barriers, and obstacles you might encounter along your path to your victory.

CHAPTER 6

The Application of SMART

"Setting goals is the first step in turning the invisible into the visible."

Tony Robbins

In this chapter, we are going to apply the SMART method of goal setting to the goal: **How to make $1,000,000 in 12 months using SMART goal setting.**

This chapter will take the SMART method of goal setting, and break it down as we consider the audacious goal of making 1 million dollars in 12 months.

The primary purpose of this chapter is to demonstrate how you can think through every letter of the acronym, in a systematic and strategic way, to help you achieve this and any other goal.

You will notice that as we work through the process of formulating the goal of making $1,000,000 in 12 months, many different factors related to goals will be brought into light. I think that usually we ignore many of these factors when we establish weak goals, which underlies the value of the SMART method of goal setting; it forces you to address several important factors which will determine whether you will achieve your goal or not.

The process in this Chapter reflects a logical and systematic way of formulating your goals. So without further ado, let's consider several ways in which you can and cannot make $1,000,000 in 12 months.

How NOT To Make $1,000,000

To begin with let me unequivocally state that there are easy and hard ways to make $1,000,000. The hard ways include methods which are generally impossible, immoral or illegal. The methods I am referring to are:

1. **Winning the lottery**. This is virtually impossible. You have a greater statistical chance of becoming the president (or prime minister) of your country, than winning the lottery. You are more likely to die driving to the ticket office in a car accident, than winning the grand prize. I would count this one out immediately.

2. **Inheriting it**. Usually you need to have a very rich relative who really loves you for this to work. Considering the vast majority of people who do not have said relatives, either rich or loving, I would count this one out too.

3. **Robbing a bank**. This is illegal and it is doubtful you will ever enjoy a penny of it. Most bank robbers get caught, and in the unlikely event they manage to dodge the authorities, live the rest of their lives looking over their shoulders. I would also knock this one off my list.

4. **Scamming Old People**. This is immoral and illegal, and downright nasty. This is a shameful and evil thing to do and I certainly hope you will never lower yourself to this level. For many people reading this Chapter, I imagine you would rather support your aging parents, than take advantage of them. This is another one I would knock off my list.

5. **Finding it**. This is also a statistical improbability and if you did find that amount of money you would most certainly have to hand it in to the authorities. This idea is probably

more likely to be found in the movies anyway, so I wouldn't regard it seriously to begin with.

How To Make $1,000,000

Okay, so now that we have discussed how you will most likely not make $1,000,000, let us consider some of the ways you can.

1. **You can earn it.** I would consider this to be the most likely manner in which you can get your hands on $1,000,000 and live to enjoy it. Through the process of earning the money, you will grow immeasurably and develop irreplaceable skills which will benefit you for the rest of your life.

2. **You can become a CEO of a major corporation**. This is a slam dunk approach, as most CEO's at this level earn far in excess of $1,000,000 per annum.

3. **You can make it trading on the stock exchange**. Many people amass millions investing on the stock market. If you have the knowledge and the skills, this is a potential winner for you.

4. **You can invent something marvellous**. Big corporations regularly buy inventions from the little guys, who go from zero to hero almost instantly. There are many stories of ordinary people who got massive pay-outs for their hobby inventions.

5. **You could start a small business.** You could develop your own product or service, which could earn you the big bucks. This Chapter focuses more on this option, as it seems to be the most likely one people will take or consider.

THE APPLICATION OF SMART
GOAL SETTING

So how do you go about making $1,000,000 in 12 months using SMART goals?

I imagine that many people who read this Chapter will be hoping for a magic bullet of some kind, which will magically cause $1,000,000 to appear without any investment of time or effort. Unfortunately, there is no fairy godmother or genie in a lamp in this story.

Magically finding said genie would also not be of any real value to you – long term that is.

What I am going to show you is not a get rich quick scheme. The good news is that it is probably the most tried and tested method to attain great success and wealth ever invented. This system can be used to achieve any goal you could ever have. There is a proverb which says, "Give a man a fish and you will feed him for a day, but teach a man to fish and you will feed his entire family for a lifetime."

So ask yourself this question: is it better to receive a big wad of cash that you can spend in a day, or receive a means to make that cash for a lifetime? I think the latter option sounds like the best one long term. How about you?

What's more, I did not intend to infer from the title of this Chapter that making $1,000,000 was going to be easy and require little or no work. I deliberately inserted the words "goal setting" to clarify that this was a process, not an outcome.

So I am going to take you through the process, but as you follow it you will need to place your own unique circumstances and situation into the process. This is, after all, your means of making $1,000,000 in 12 months, so you need to own it.

This method of goal setting does not just apply to making $1,000,000 in 12 months; it can be applied to a host of other goals too. These could include:

- Finding a suitable job

- Buying your first home

- Losing weight

- Getting fit to run a marathon

- Passing a University degree, or getting a PhD

- Buying a new car

- Spending more time with your kids

- Going on an overseas holiday

Let's get back to the goal of making $1 million dollars in 12 months. When we use the SMART method, we have to check that our goal meets certain quality standards. As you might know, SMART stands for

- **S - Specific**
- **M - Measurable**
- **A – Achievable/Actionable**
- **R - Realistic/Relevant**
- **T - Time Frame**

WORKING THROUGH SMART

Be Specific

Is the goal "I want to make $1,000,000 in 12 months" specific?

Does it contain enough information to allow us to understand what it is?

On the surface of it, it looks quite clear. We want to make $1 million in 12 months.

However, the goal lacks specific information about how we are going to make that amount of money. We will leave that issue for the moment, as the 'how' part will come, as we progress through the process.

Note: It is vitally important at this point not to get hung up on the 'how' part of the process; for now just focus on the 'what'.

Measurable

Yes this goal is measurable. $1,000,000 is a very specific amount of money. It can be counted. It can be weighed on a scale. It can be visually seen in your bank account.

The time you have allocated to your goal is also very measurable; 12 months can be counted down. Your time frame consists of 52 weeks, or 365 days. This information will prove to be very useful as you plan your strategy to $1,000,000.

Achievable

I think this is a little bit more difficult to answer.

What is achievable for you may not be achievable for me! We all have different skills, talents and abilities. We have all developed particular biases and beliefs. All these factors will determine how we view the achievability of a particular goal.

Napoleon Hill once said, "What the mind can conceive, it can achieve." If you believe you can achieve $1,000,000 in 12 months, then you can achieve it. If you doubt it, then you will fail.

Has anyone else ever achieved this goal?

Before you consider how achievable this goal is for you personally, ask yourself this question: has anyone else in history achieved this goal before? Has any other human being been able to make $1 million in 12 months?

I think you will agree with me, that there are practically millions of examples of people who make $1,000,000 per annum. Most CEO's of major corporations earn far more than that.

The website http://www.aflcio.org, publishes the top 100 highest paid CEO's. For example, Joe Kiani from Masimo Corp earned $119,222,614 in 2015, while Timothy Walbert of Horizon Pharma Plc earned $93,379,077 in 2015. These people didn't just earn $1 million in 12 months, they earned amounts far in excess of that.[1]

On the list of the top earning CEO's, the range of earnings was also far in excess of a paltry $1,000,000. The highest paid CEO earned $119,222,614 while the lowest earned $18,931,068.

In a recent article featured on CNBC, it was stated that there are now over 10.4 million American households with assets of $1 million or more, which does not include their main residence.[34] This number keeps growing annually, even in tougher economic times, as becoming a millionaire has become easier to achieve than ever before. These people do not necessarily earn $1,000,000 per year, but if they cashed in all their assets (not including the home they occupy) they would have over $1 million in the bank.

So to answer the question, has anybody else on the planet achieved $1,000,000 in 12 months, the answer is a resounding yes. Many have – and you could be one of them too.

So the next question to ask yourself: Am I able to earn $1,000,000 in the next 12 months?

One way to answer this question is to ask yourself if you have ever earned $1,000,000 in 12 months before. The logic is, if you have done it before, you can do it again. But if you haven't, you are not alone, as most people would have never even come close to earning this amount in one year.

Statistically, most of the world's population does not make anything near that amount per annum. Billions of people will probably never get close to that figure ever, even over their entire life time. They just earn too little. It is a sad fact, but true.

It is estimated that in 1990, 1.9 billion people, roughly 43% of people living in the developing world, lived on less than $1.25 US per day. In 2008, that figure fell to 22% of the population or roughly 1.3 billion people.[3] That's a phenomenal amount of people who earn very little, and this truly shows how disproportionately wealth is spread among the citizens of the world.

Even in developed countries the average annual income is not anywhere near $1 Million per annum. For example the annual wage in the USA in 2014 was $46,481.52, according to an official social security website.[71] This means that if the average citizen of the USA was able to save every cent they earned annually, they would need 21 years to amass $1,000,000. Most people spend more than they earn each year. This goal is an impossible undertaking for most people, particularly if you earn an ordinary income.

Statistically, most people reading this Chapter will probably never have earned anywhere near $1,000,000 per annum at any time in their life, and unless they make some radical shift in how they approach their goals, never will.

Is this goal really achievable, or is it just a pipe dream?

Before you throw your hands up in despair and give up, realise one thing: only 3 – 8% of the world's population set and pursue goals. They are also some of the richest and most successful people. If you take a closer look at their strategies you will note that goal setting is a key part of their approach.

The simple truth is if you haven't achieved success in acquiring significant wealth, it might be that you have not been using the right tools or utilising the correct thinking. Changing your approach may change the game significantly.

Okay, so maybe I have convinced you (or maybe not!) that you too can enter the ranks of individuals who have scaled the $1,000,000 per annum mountain. Before we pop out the bubbly and start celebrating, let's take a look at some key figures related to making $1,000,000.

There are 52 weeks in a year, so taking 4 weeks off for holidays we have 48 weeks left to make $1,000,000.

If we divide $1,000,000/48 weeks we have to earn $20,833.33 per week.

If we take $20,833.33/40 hour work week we get $520.83 per hour.

So to make $1,000,000 in 12 months you will have to earn $520.83 minimum per hour, assuming a 40 hour workweek over 48 weeks.

Now that is a sizeable amount of money; an impossibly large figure for most. There are of course some professions which charge hourly rates close to that and above that level. These include

- Medical specialists
- Plastic surgeons
- Attorneys
- Coaches
- Consultants

For most individuals, this will probably seem like an impossible figure to attain, particularly if they have only been earning minimum wage, or an average income their entire life.

The amounts I have shown you above are actual profit. It does not take into consideration taxes, expenses, salaries, personal drawings and the like. You will still need to live and pay yourself an income over the 12 months. If you want $1,000,000 at the end of the 12 months then you will have to turnover a whole lot more.

From what I have shown you above, I imagine most people would be discounting their chances at this point of ever reaching the $1,000,000 threshold. Hold on for a moment; don't go down that rabbit hole yet. There may still be hope.

Hence this brings us to our next letter R

Realistic

Is this goal realistic or is it just pie in the sky?

Personally, I think it is entirely realistic and doable, because there are thousands of people doing it every day. A key step will be to set the right goal, break it down into sub goals, and achieve them one at a time. Let me show you a few examples of how you can do this.

Example 1

Recently I got sent an invitation to enroll in an online course on internet marketing (IM). The course ran for 6 weeks and covered every topic imaginable related to successful IM. The course was completely comprehensive and catered for every contingency. The course clearly provided great value for the cost. The price for enrollment was $997.

The course creator would have spent months creating the course. Let's say he spent 11 months designing the videos and materials. Near the launch date, he started promoting the program and gathering respondents. As a professional marketer, he already knew where to go looking for the right participants and where to find people most likely to register. He set up relationships with other business owners who gave him access to their email lists for a commission. He used social media connections and very specific online advertising campaigns.

By the time the launch date arrived he had over 1,500 eager people enrolled and ready to take the course.

After 11 months of hard work designing the course, as the 12 month ticked over, he had made over $1,000,000 in turnover. His profit would have been high, because the course was delivered entirely electronically.

I gave you this example to help shift your perception on how to earn money. This approach moves from earning money on an hourly basis, to selling a product and using technology to automate the process.

We all know that you can only earn a finite amount of money in one hour. But the example above shifts that thinking to a whole new level. Changing your perception about your predicament can open your thinking up to an entire new world of opportunities.

Example 2

Recently, I heard another example on how to make a million dollars in 12 months. This example illustrates the aspect of incremental goal setting really well. It clearly shows the power of setting step by step incremental goals.

The goal of making $1,000,000 in 12 months is a long term goal, and unless you change your focus to smaller incremental goals you might end up self-sabotaging the goal altogether. Most people won't be able to produce a workable idea on how to make $1,000,000 in a single step. So they give up from the get go.

This is the wrong approach, because the jump from $0 to $1,000,000 is too large a jump to make in a single hop.

A much better approach is to step back and think about an idea which will help you earn just $10 for instance. Instead of trying to come up with a strategy to earn $1,000,000 think about how you can earn just $10. It doesn't matter if you sell an item or a service for $10 apiece. This should be relatively easy to do. You could wash cars, windows, mow lawns or paint fences, write an eBook, make a training video or audio tape. There are endless opportunities to make $10. Once you have an idea, you act on it and produce the product or service (this is your first sub-goal).

For example let's say you made a basic 30 minute training video. You produce the video for $2 and sell it for $12, making a $10 profit. You take your product around your neighbourhood and sell 10 copies to local residents. Presto, you have earned $100, but more importantly found an idea that makes $100. You have achieved your first goal.

Now you can repeat the system 10 more times to earn $1000. So now you have a system that makes $1000. The problem is that you cannot keep doing this all by yourself as you don't have enough time in the day. You need to step things up a notch and employ what is known as leverage.

To leverage your system, you can do any number of things. You could hire 10 people and pay them a commission to sell your product, or you could sell your product online as a digital download, etc.

Ultimately, you need to find a system which is able to repeat your $1000 system 10 times. When you discover this you will have found a system that makes $10,000.

Repeat that system 10 more times and you have a system that makes $100,000. You guessed it, if you repeat this system 10 more times you have a system that makes you $1,000,000.

Each step in the process is a sub-goal of your primary goal. Each step is achievable and manageable. Each step helps you climb the ladder towards your No 1 Goal .

But notice, that the whole system started with a small step of making just $10.

The point is not to despise small beginnings. To achieve your long term goals you need to be realistic and set small easily achievable goals first.

You don't need to know how to earn $500 per hour to make a million

Goal setting is the process which takes you from $0 to $1,000,000. It starts with a basic step, which once achieved leads to the next step. You don't need to know how to earn $500 - $600 per hour, you only need to know how to earn $10 or $15. Don't get hung up on the goals several steps away, focus on the goal right in front of you first. Note: Make sure your step can be leveraged.

Once you achieve that one you will be ready for the next one

If you can't achieve the current step, you will not be able to get to the next one. Sure sometimes you can jump steps, but in most instances steps will be too large to jump. You will have to achieve each step sequentially and systematically.

The beauty of this process is that the solutions present themselves when you need them. At step 1 you need a solution for a $10 product or service. Not a solution for a $1000 product or service.

If you prefer, step 1 could be a $1000 product or service. There is no rule that says it must be a $10 offer. It might be a much harder prospect to come up with a $1000 offer as opposed to a $10 offer.

Again, let me reiterate, don't get hung up on the goal several steps away. Focus on the step in front of you and find a solution for that one first.

Relevant

Now let's discuss Goal Relevance.

Not everyone wants to make $1,000,000. There are many people in our world who would rather just scrape by and live a basic simple life. They are not remotely interested in making a $1,000,000 in 12 months or any other time frame. This goal does not hold much relevance for them.

Yet another person may be on the brink of bankruptcy. The bank might be ready to foreclose on their house, the car dealership reclaim the car, and the furniture company take back the lounge suite. To this person making $1,000,000 holds high relevancy. The money will help solve their financial doom, and get them out of the hole they find themselves in.

Still for others, they don't really need the money. They have enough to get by tomorrow, the next day and the next. They are comfortable enough, they do not have to set and pursue a goal of making a million dollars.

So where do you sit? How relevant is making a $1,000,000 to you?

You seriously need to answer this question if you have any hope of pursuing such an audacious goal.

One way to know this is to ask yourself if this goal is consistent with your values and beliefs. If it is not, then you will have an uphill battle setting and pursuing this goal. Not everyone will be comfortable with setting a goal like this, and you can only answer that for yourself by looking inwards and discerning what's important to you.

Time Frame

The final consideration you need to make concerning your goal is whether it has a valid time frame. As you can see your goal has a clearly defined time frame of 12 months, or 365 days.

The time frame should be long enough to give you ample opportunity to achieve success, but not too long that it wastes time unnecessarily. Likewise, the timeframe should not be so short that you cannot successfully complete the goal.

For some people, 12 months would be way too long. Imagine someone like Bill Gates or Warren Buffett. They can earn $1 Million in less than a day. But, for someone who lives on less than $2 per day, it will take 500,000 days to accumulate $1,000,000; a time frame ridiculously too large to contemplate.

Time frames are important considerations, as they push us to work towards our goals; if we didn't set them, we would just drift along. Drifting happens to be a common ailment affecting most of the human population.

Now that you have considered the deeper aspects of making $1,000,000 in 12 months it is time to apply a few goal setting guidelines to get the ball rolling – assuming of course that you have decided this is something you want to do.

Set Long And Short Term Goals

The goal we have been discussing so far is what is called a long term goal. To achieve it you will need to set several short term goals. In the table below I have given you an example of both. The example follows the previous idea where an entrepreneur made a video which he sold for $12 and earned a $10 profit.

Goal	Short Term Goals	Long Term Goals
1	Develop an idea on how to make $10 per sale (profit)	Make $1,000,000 by completing short term goals 1 - 6
2	Make $100 by repeating goal 1 ten times	
3	Make $1,000 by repeating goal 2 ten times	

4	Make $10,000 by repeating goal 3 ten times
5	Make $100,000 by repeating goal 4 ten times
6	Make $1,000,000 by repeating goal 5 ten times

MOTIVATION

Once you have your goal set you should list as many reasons as possible for why you want to achieve this goal.

If you cannot list 40 or 50 good reasons, maybe the goal is not that important to you. The more reasons you can list the clearer it will become that this is something you truly want.

Why Do You Want This Goal?

List as many reasons as possible, why you want to achieve this goal in the first place. Examples could be:

✓ To be financially independent

✓ To pay off my house; to buy a house

✓ To prepare for my retirement

✓ To pay of my mounting debts and get out of becoming bankrupt

✓ To resign from my job which I can't stand

✓ To invest in the stock market

✓ To pay for medical treatment

✓ To give my kids an education

✓ To provide for my aging parents

✓ To start my own business

Once you have listed off every conceivable reason you can think of, you will have either convinced yourself that this is something you truly want or you will have realised this is not what you want after all. Either way, you are in a better position. You have gained more insight and are that much closer to discovering your purpose and mission.

Let's assume this is a goal you truly desire. The next task is to list off every step you will have to take to reach your goal. Examples could be:

List every step you need to take to achieve your goal

✓ Research products and services I could provide or produce

✓ Put together a business plan

✓ Assess my skills and knowledge

✓ Develop a product or service I can sell

✓ Get necessary training and advice

✓ Set long term goals

✓ Set short term goals

Many of these steps will become your sub-goals. You will need to systematically achieve each sub-goal to climb the ladder towards your major goal.

Other Considerations

You will most likely also require several resources, extra training, various contacts and help from family, friends and other professionals. You will also have to assess the many barriers and obstacles both personal and professional, you will have to face.

What resources will you need

- ✓ Office space
- ✓ A car
- ✓ A phone
- ✓ A website

What skills and training do you need

- ✓ Writing skills
- ✓ Administration skills
- ✓ Financial planning skills
- ✓ Communication skills
- ✓ Technical skills

What people and contacts will you need

- ✓ Legal advisor
- ✓ Accountant
- ✓ Web designer
- ✓ Small business advisor
- ✓ Personal coach

What barriers/obstacles will you need to overcome

- ✓ Lack of persistence
- ✓ Lack of self-discipline

✓ Lack of technical know how

✓ Competition

✓ Lack of capital

✓ Lack of motivation

These are all important questions to address when you are planning your goal.

Tom Landry said, "Setting a goal is not the main thing. It is deciding how you will go about achieving it and staying with that plan."

Goal setting is not just about writing down what it is you want to achieve, it is, more importantly, about planning how you will do it and then staying with that plan.

Each major goal you attempt will be a new mountain you must climb. You need strategies, tactics and schemes to reach the summit.

What's Your Tactical Plan

Nobody tries to scale Mt Everest without a tactical plan – to do so would be suicide. Rather you would consider important factors such as: which time of the year to make the attempt, where to camp out on each day, which face to approach the summit from, how much oxygen to carry, and so on. Without tactics, strategies and plans you will be bound to fail, or worse, die.

Your approach to make $1,000,000 in 12 months needs to be the same. Don't go into it blindfolded. There is no way to reach this summit without a plan, and preparation. But reach the summit you can. Many of the people who attempt Mt Everest reach the summit. Many do not. Planning and preparation go a long way to making it to the top.

So there you have it. You are now at base camp 1. The mountain is ahead of you. You can see the peak in distance. You feel excited, exhilarated and afraid. You can only make it to the top if you take the first step. Now take it.

KEY POINTS TO REMEMBER

- Many people want to be rich, but few take the time to seriously think through what it might take to do so.

- There is a big difference between wishing for great wealth and actually attaining it. The real difference lies in the establishment of your goals, and the quality of your planning.

- Once you have taken the desire in your mind and applied it to paper, you begin the process of considering the various components which can make your goal a reality.

- Following the SMART method will help you gain a clearer perspective on what it takes to achieve a particular goal.

- Achieving $1 million dollars in 12 months is an audacious goal which for most people will be very difficult to achieve. It is not impossible, nor out of the reach of anyone who establishes a plan, and then works that plan with persistence and determination.

CHAPTER 7

Psychological Tactics: Using The Power of the Subconscious

"Our subconscious minds have no sense of humor, play no jokes and cannot tell the difference between reality and an imagined thought or image. What we continually think about eventually will manifest in our lives."
Robert Collier

You are probably the most complex of all living creatures in the universe. You have been fitted with one of the most extraordinary and marvellous devices in all of creation: your brain.

For decades, computer scientists have tried to build a better machine than your brain, and even though they have succeeded in building supercomputers which can process data faster, these still pale in comparison to the simplicity and sleek design of the human brain. For instance, your brain runs on the power it takes to light a small dimly lit bulb, whereas the Fujitsu supercomputer, K, sucks up an enormous amount of power which could light 10,000 homes. Even a cats brain makes the newest iPad look stupid. A cats brain can store 1,000 times more data and processes that data a million times faster.[5]

Your brain is the control centre for your entire body, yet it weighs a mere 2% of your total body weight. It consumes more than 20% of your energy and oxygen. It is made up of 73% water and if it gets just 2% dehydrated, it will begin to affect your attention, memory and other cognitive skills. Your amount of willpower is linked to this energy state, which means your willpower will be lower when your energy or oxygen levels are lower.

Your brain has a vast number of brain cells, the exact number is unknown, but rough estimates suggest that the average brain has approximately 86 to 100 billion neurons. Each neuron has around 40,000 synaptic connections to other neurons. To put this into perspective, a piece of brain tissue the size of a grain of sand has 100,000 neurons and over 1 billion synaptic connections to other cells. Information between neurons travels faster than a formula one racing car. There are over 10,000 different types of neurons in your brain and over 100,000 chemical reactions taking place every second. You also have another brain, other than the one in your head. There is a "second brain" in your intestines that contains around 100,000 neurons.

But, the true mind blowing aspect of your brain relates to how it can be wired up. There are around 10 to the power of 60 atoms in the known universe (10 with 60 zeros behind it e.g. 10,000,000 + 54 more 0's), whereas your brain has 10 to the power of 1,000,000 different ways to wire itself up (10 with 1 million zeroes behind it). This number is so immense that we are unable to comprehend its enormity. Nonetheless your brain is capable of this astonishing feat.

By the time you reach 25 years of age, your brain will have reached full maturity. Up until then it is in constant flux, adding and subtracting vast numbers of connections and pruning itself relentlessly.

The average brain generates around 50,000 – 70,000 thoughts per day, that's about 42 thoughts per minute, or roughly 1 thought every 1.5 seconds. Unfortunately, for most people 70% of these thoughts are negative. A thought is similar to a physical pathway which you travel over continuously, eventually forming a deep groove, which makes transmission over the same ground easier in the future. So if you continue to have negative thoughts, these pathways will become well-trodden and dominate your thinking.

Brain size is not an indication of intelligence. Albert Einstein's brain weighed 2.71 pounds (1,230 grams), which is 10% smaller than the average person's brain (3 pounds/1,400 grams). One big difference found in Einstein's brain was that it had a higher density of neurons compared to the average brain.

Even though we now live in the information age, some sources suggest we are not getting any smarter. Since the Victorian era, average intelligence has been in decline, down 1.6 points per decade for a total of 13.35 points. Our attention spans are also in decline. At the turn of the century (2000), the average attention span was 12 seconds, but now it is 8 seconds. The average goldfish attention span is 9 seconds.

Your brain has vast storage potential, virtually unlimited. It doesn't get used up like computer RAM, hence have the capacity to learn unlimited amounts of information. You can learn until you die, but your death is not an indication of having reached learning capacity.

You are not in full control of your life. Almost 95% of all decisions are made in the subconscious mind. The decisions which pop into your head have been made unbeknownst to your conscious awareness. They have been processed behind the scenes, at blazing speeds, and you discover them when they enter your consciousness.

So why am I telling you all this? Because I want you to realise the incredible potential you possess. You are a marvel of creation, a wonder of the universe. You have been fitted with the most amazing device known to mankind, and the only difference between achieving your best self or drifting into oblivion, is how you choose to use it.

Automatic Thinking

How many times have you driven home from work, only to discover when you arrive home that you have no actual recollection of the trip? It seemed as if you switched onto auto pilot when you left work and then switched it off again when you arrived home. One moment you remember getting into the car, the next you are getting out.

During the many times we complete a task like driving home, we are not processing very much new (novel information), so the trip goes by without us noticing much about it. When we complete everyday tasks like this, we simply rerun well-rehearsed memory scripts we have imprinted in our minds. We enter into a type of mindless state and proceed to think about other things which grab our attention.

It's a type of stereotypical re-enactment, because these situations are very common, and so well understood that you automatically perform what you need to and don't pay much attention to the details.

There is a large body of research which points to this aspect of mindlessness. For example a classic study done by, Langer and colleagues (1978) highlighted how mindlessly people respond to requests. When tasks are small, people pay very little attention to the details of requests, but as task demands increase, so do people's attention to them. The researchers showed that pushing into a line to get photocopies done is easier and elicits less attention when the requestor only has 5 copies to make. When task requirements increase, people pay more attention to the excuses you give for the intrusion.[52]

The researchers showed that you can give just about any ridiculous reason to push in and make 5 copies because the task is small, but you need to be more careful when the task demands increase, like making 20 copies because then people pay more attention to the details of the request.

The fact is, we tend to wade through life in a type of mental lull and waft from one situation to another not paying much attention to what's going on around us. So unless a situation jars us from this mental sleepwalking, the world just drifts on by without us noticing.

But this is understandable because we tend to automate the many repetitive day to day tasks and processes we live by and store these as scripts in our subconscious minds. This has the benefit of freeing up our conscious minds to focus on more novel and important things and situations. Mindlessness has its advantages, and like Langer suggests, this ability to tune out from daily repetitive tasks is more of an achievement than a dilemma. It is an efficient way of handling the millions of bits of information streaming through our senses and into our brains on a daily basis.

Every day we are hit with a type of stimulus bombardment, which is getting worse as time goes by, as today more than ever we have to deal with the constant wave of interruptions designed to grab our attention. The airwaves have become saturated with media messages vying for our limited attention. For instance, my cell phone would like nothing more than to emit a continuous string of beeps to notify me of updates to my social profiles, new emails arriving or some other non-essential. All of these interruptions jar us from our work and disrupt our concentration. And yes there is a cost involved, as it takes cognitive energy to regain your focus.

Introducing The Reticular Activating System

How do we manage the countless bits of information lining up to gain access to our attention, without driving us completely nuts? Introducing the Reticular Activation System (RAS), which is a small network of nerves situated at the base of the skull.

This remarkable part of the brain acts like a type of filter which controls what gets access to our brains. It is not much different from the functions provided by a secretary. A secretary controls who gets access to the boss. The same functions are provided by a bouncer, who lets certain desirables in and keeps others out of a night club.

The reticular activating system (RAS) is the gateway to the brain through which all sensory information travels. Your sense of smell is the only exception because it has a direct link to the brain's emotional centre. The RAS is responsible for what you are paying attention to right now, and what environmental factors are currently arousing your attention.

The RAS will quickly respond to the sound of your name, and is also highly sensitive to noticing any information which would threaten your wellbeing. So it is naturally attuned to some things. Fortunately to a large degree we have control on what we can choose to tune our RAS into.

It is very useful when you are looking for something in particular in the grocery store. For example, the other day my wife asked me to pick up some BBQ sauce from the supermarket on my way home. I wasn't completely sure where the BBQ sauce was, or what aisle it was in. I went searching by walking up and down the aisles, rapidly scanning the contents of the shelves as I went by.

My RAS was programmed to look for BBQ sauce so everything that was not BBQ sauce was filtered out of my attention.

Eventually I spotted it on the lower shelf of Isle 2. If you asked me where the baked beans were, I wouldn't know even though I had walked right past them and looked straight at them. At that moment in time my filtering system was not interested in baked beans so it blocked that item from registering on my attention.

Other examples abound of times when your attention is switched onto a particular object and then you start noticing the thing popping up all over the place. If one day you suddenly fancy a certain motor car, say a BMW 3 Series Sports, and happen to take one out for a test drive, or look it up on the internet, chances are good you will start seeing them popping up all over the place. As you drive around town you will begin to notice how many BMW 3 Series Sports there are. You will be surprised to find them appearing all over the place and probably wonder why you didn't see them before.

Your Reticular Activation System is a highly efficient system as it limits what information gets passed down the line, and only filters through relevant bits of information into your awareness. Only once you have programmed your RAS to filter through particular bits of information, will you become aware of them.

As I stated in the introduction, humans by default are wired to filter through more negative information than positive. Out of the 50,000 – 70,000 thoughts generated every day, 70% are negative. This may be the default setting, but it does not need to stay that way. You can change your thinking, and thereby change your life. If you start training your mind to focus on more positive and uplifting thoughts, you will configure your RAS to start noticing and filtering in more positive stimuli from the world around you. You will start seeing the beauty and wonder in the world more clearly.

For example, there is a saying that two men in a prison cell were one night looking out the window. One man saw stars while the other saw bars. They were both in the same location, looking at the night's sky from the same vantage point. Yet one man saw freedom, wonder, amazement, joy, and hope, while the other saw prison, privation, depression, suffering, and pain. One man's RAS was set to let through positivity, while another negativity. One man had his filter tuned to freedom while the other to incarceration.

What frequency do you have your RAS set to?

When it comes to goal setting, you can tune your RAS to your most important goals. It will not come naturally, as humans we have a inbuilt propensity to more easily spot the negative aspects in our environments. To achieve your best self, you will need to continually tune your RAS to your highest goals, so that they form deep, well-trodden groves into your subconscious mind. Later on in this Chapter, I will show you a tool to help you achieve this objective.

We Have Set Limitations

Our mental faculties associated with awareness (our conscious mind) have set limitations. Some research suggests we can hold 5 to 9 pieces information in our awareness at any one time.[57] While in contrast our subconscious minds seem to have an extraordinarily large memory capacity, capable of storing incalculable amounts of data.

Exercise 1

To highlight this aspect of limited attention, take a moment to experience how limited your cognitive awareness really is. Stop reading this Chapter right now, and take a moment to listen to all the sounds around you. Count the number of sounds you can hear which you were scarcely aware off a few moments ago.

Do that now for 60 seconds…

Did you notice a tick-tock of the clock hanging on the wall, or the tweeting of a small sparrow outside your window? Possibly you became aware of the drone of the traffic outside, or the helicopter flying overhead. Maybe it's the muffled sound of the people talking in the room next door, or the faint barking of a dog in the distance.

These sounds just a moment ago were non-existent, as far as your conscious awareness was concerned, but now they have become real – they have entered into your reality. They have taken shape in your consciousness. Things become real when you notice them and when you give them your attention.

Exercise 2

Now take a complete 360 degree panoramic view around the room you are sitting in, and pick out anything and everything you see which is black, counting them as you go.

Do that now before reading on…

Now close your eyes and without looking around the room again, list off everything you saw which was white.

Okay, now open your eyes and take a look and see which items you got right and which ones you missed. How well did you do?

Naturally the task is made more or less easy based on how many objects there are in the room and how familiar you are with the space.

The point is that you can only be aware of so much information at any one time. Your conscious awareness has limited capacity.

Fortunately, your subconscious mind is unmatched by the amount of information it can process and store. It is a huge, vast expanse of synaptic connections, constantly connecting and disconnecting neurons throughout the grey matter in your head. It is a wonderful and incomprehensible creation, and you can use this innate power you already have to achieve your highest and grandest objectives.

What counts is what you feed into your mind. This is where the real difference is made between successful people and those who achieve very little with their lives. Successful people feed their minds with success enhancing thoughts, they focus on their goals and chase after their dreams. They use their mental facilities in a way which promotes their personal growth and development. They leverage both their conscious and subconscious minds to their fullest potential.

The Law Of Attraction

The Law of Attraction has been around for quite some time and has been made popular in several self-help books, movies, audio programs and famous people who have espoused its utility. But it also has its critics.

The Law of Attraction states that you will attract into your life the things you think about most of the time. You will draw into your reality those people, objects and circumstances you give your attention to. Whatever you focus on will begin to emerge in the world around you.

But a word of caution, the Law of Attraction is unbiased, it does not care whether you think good or bad thoughts, it simply acts on the thoughts you have. So if you think about disease, poverty, lack, or pain most of the time, you will discover these things will begin to dominate your life.

If you focus your attention on health, wealth, good relationships, and happiness, this is the reality you will begin to experience. The Law of Attraction relates to your dominant thoughts. It is closely linked to the patterns of thinking which persist in your mind on a daily basis.

The Law of Attraction is not a natural law like the Law of Gravity or the Law of Cause and Effect. There is no mention of it in Psychological texts. If you don't believe me consult any University Psychology Text and try and find it in the index. It's just not there – believe me I have looked (I have a PhD in Psychology so I have quite a few Psychological textbooks).

Nonetheless, the Law of Attraction does capture actual psychological phenomena which demonstrate how our thinking affects how we live our lives. Understanding some of these components of thinking is useful when you desire to align your mind with your goals.

The Self-Fulfilling Prophesy

For example, one particular psychosocial phenomenon which has garnered significant psychological research is the self-fulfilling prophesy.

A self-fulfilling prophesy is a prediction that in a sense makes itself come true. This effect was confirmed way back in the 1960's when two researches Robert Rosenthal and Lenore Jacobson conducted their classic research study on elementary school teachers.[68] They went to an elementary school to conduct IQ tests on all the students. Thereafter they randomly selected names and proceeded to tell teachers that the children whose names they had selected were about to "bloom" academically.

Naturally, this was not true as the student names were chosen randomly; the truth was that Rosenthal and Jacobson had no idea which students would bloom and which ones wouldn't. Eight months later they returned to the school and tested the students again. They discovered that the ones they said were "bloomers" showed significant improvements on their IQ tests compared to the "non-bloomers".

They expected this would happen, because they assumed teachers would begin to treat the "bloomers" differently after they were told that these students were more gifted academically. This is exactly what had happened. Teachers had given these students more attention, more feedback, more challenging tasks and more opportunities to respond in class. They had effectively made the self-fulfilling prophesy a reality.

Since then, further research has discovered that the phenomena of self-fulfilling prophesy is prevalent in many other domains. When you believe something to be true you begin to behave in a way that makes it true.

What Do You Believe

The self-fulfilling prophesy is a type of belief you hold concerning a future outcome. That outcome can be either positive or negative. Our beliefs are incredibly powerful, because we align our behaviour to be consistent with them. What you believe drives your actions.

Anthony Robbins eloquently states, "If you raise your standards but don't really believe you can meet them, you've already sabotaged yourself. You won't even try; you'll be lacking the sense of certainty that allows you to tap the deepest capacity that's within you... Our beliefs are like unquestioned commands, telling us how things are, what's possible and impossible and what we can and cannot do. They shape every action, every thought and every feeling that we experience. As a result, changing our belief systems is central to making any real and lasting change in our lives."[65]

If you believe you are poor, sick, unlikeable, lonely and hopeless, then you will live in a way that is consistent with that belief. When you discover that those are the exact circumstances you find yourself in, then you will have made your belief come true. You will have proved your prediction correct. You can pat yourself on the back and say, "see I knew it was true!" But this to no avail, because you will have achieved the opposite to what you truly want, which is to be healthy, loved, happy and successful.

To achieve your goals and realise the positive outcomes you richly desire, you will have to change your beliefs about your future, and thereby change the way you live your life.

Pablo Picasso once said, "He can who thinks he can, he can't who thinks he can't." Before scientists ever ran studies to support this, Picasso already knew it, because it was so prevalent in the world around him. Picasso noticed that the people who believed they could achieve their dreams did so, while those who lacked belief achieved very little.

Likewise Henry Ford understood this principle when he said, "Think you can, think you can't, either way you'll be right." Ford obviously had witnessed it enough times to realise that people define their own limits by the thoughts they nurture and impress on their minds. Ford failed several times in business before eventually succeeding. He had a unstoppable drive to succeed and failure was simply not an option.

Interestingly, research shows that some people put the power of self-fulfilling prophesies to good use. Feingold (1992) found that people who viewed themselves as being more attractive, reported higher levels of extroversion, social comfort and mental health than those who were less comfortable with their appearance. This could be a good example of the self-fulfilling prophesy at work, because people who believed they were more attractive engaged in more attractive enhancing behaviours, like smiling, for example which enhances a person's attractiveness.[53] Your beliefs cause you to behave in a way which are consistent with your mental thoughts and feelings.

Thoughts Become Things

In Napoleon Hill's book, "think and grow rich," [42] Hill makes an interesting point about thoughts. According to Hill, thoughts become things. On the surface of it, this rings with notions of fairy tales. You get a picture of a fairy godmother waving her wand and materialising something wonderful out of thin air. But the reality is that just thinking about something does not materialise it, at least not for us mere mortals.

A thought can become a thing when it is acted upon. An artist starts a great painting by first visualising a beautiful portrait in his mind's eye. Thereafter he places his canvas on an easel, pulls out his paints and brushes, and begins the meticulous process of materialising his mental image onto the canvas. What he doesn't do is visualise it in his mind and transfer that picture magically to the canvas.

Every other undertaking follows the exact same process. A mental image is acted upon and something appears. Thoughts do become things. But the universe does not magically materialise your imaginings into objects. The Mercedes Benz does not simply appear in the driveway one day because you close your eyes, visualise it and when you open your eyes again, there it is, with keys in the ignition and a big red bow tied around it. You don't lose 20kg overnight because you just have a mental image of a thinner body, nor do you stare at the exam paper and see the answers magically appear (though I know a lot of students who would be happy if this were the case). Thoughts can only take on physical properties when you act on them. Thoughts in the absence of action are feeble.

The Law of Attraction can serve you if you realise that your most dominant thoughts are causing you to act in a certain way. Without even realising it, you act in ways which are consistent with your dominant thoughts. It is not by coincidence that you have the life you have, be that good or bad. You dominated your thinking with certain types of thoughts and consequently spent much of your time pursuing them. You get what you think about most of the time. This poem sums it up quite eloquently.

Be Careful of your thoughts

Be careful of your thoughts,
For your thoughts become your words.

Be careful of your words,
For your words become your deeds.

Be careful of your deeds,
For your deeds become your habits.

Be careful of your habits,
For your habits become your character.

Be careful of your character,
For your character becomes your destiny.

Confirmation Bias

Another psychological phenomenon which has garnered scientific scrutiny is the confirmation bias. This is the tendency for people to search for information to confirm what they already believe, and downplaying evidence which contradicts it. For example, scientists can be quite susceptible to this effect which causes them to use only hypothesis and methods to test theories which are consistent with their current thinking. You can think of the confirmation bias as a type of "yes man" which echoes back to you what you already personally believe.

If you look closely, you can notice the confirmation bias at work in many situations in the real world. For instance a student gets an assignment to write an essay on a particular topic. She goes off and does some research, but finds her primary interest is for information which has a particular slant. She avoids looking for alternative or contradictory points of view.

Later, when she gets her paper back, she is disappointed to find her feedback not as positive as she thought it would be. According to her teacher she only provided one point of view and completely ignored other competing and contradictory accounts.

The confirmation bias can cause the following problems:

- Keeps you stuck in a rut.

- Makes you reluctant to search for alternative solutions, or new theories.

- Sticks with the status quo.

- Traps you in wrong thinking.

HOW IS THIS RELEVANT TO ACHIEVING YOUR BEST SELF

The material I have presented above is highly relevant to goal achievement. Here is a basic summary of what you have just learnt and how you can apply it to getting what you richly desire in life.

1. Much of your thinking is automatic.

2. Once you learn something new your subconscious takes over running the routine, while your conscious mind is free to work on new things.

3. The thoughts which dominate your subconscious mind affect your behaviour. You automatically pursue the objects of your thinking, be they positive or negative.

4. You can program your mind by habitually doing the same things over and over again, forming habits.

5. Once habits have taken root, they live in the subconscious mind, outside of your awareness, free to run on autopilot pursuing your highest priorities.

6. You begin to notice your world becoming populated by the objects, people and places, as you start attracting them into your life because you are giving them your attention and focus.

Do you see the ramifications of this process? If you habituate the thinking process directed towards you achieving your goals you can automate the process of goal pursuit. If your goals dominate your thinking, either consciously or unconsciously, you will find yourself working to achieve them on a constant basis.

You won't be able to help yourself. You will find yourself thinking about new ideas, looking for new opportunities, accessing your creative mind to come up with solutions, doing different things, trying new approaches, always working towards your desired end. You will be driven to succeed as long as your dominant, persistent thoughts are consistent with your goals.

Personally, I think this is wonderful news for anyone who wants to improve their life but feels stuck and unable to make the changes they richly desire. However, this is all very interesting, but how do you go about automating this process to make it a reality? The answer is by keeping a Goal Achievement Journal.

One of the most important tools you can use to program your subconscious is to keep a journal. I have created The Goal Achievers Journal for this very purpose. I designed this tool with the sole purpose of helping you program your subconscious mind with your highest goals and most important priorities.

The process of journaling has many psychological and physical benefits. It has been supported by several studies, past and present. Here are just a few of the good reasons why you should embrace this practice, starting today:

146

1. Journaling improves your IQ

There are many different types of intelligence measures. One of them relates to how well you use vocabulary. You can improve your intelligence by improving your use of vocabulary. How? By learning more words, and integrating them into your writing, speaking, and thinking.

One report coming out of the University of Victoria suggests that, "Writing as part of language learning has a positive correlation with intelligence."[31]

If you spent more time writing every day, you will increase your intelligence. You will become smarter and develop greater brainpower.

With access to more words and a wider vocabulary, your thoughts will be richer, fuller and more able to express and articulate your dreams and desires – particularly in your writing. This will provide you with more clarity. You will become more focused and pursue your goals with more precision.

2. Journaling will help you achieve your goals

When you continually write out your dreams and desires you program your subconscious mind with images of what you want to achieve. This activates your reticular activating system (RAS), which builds a filter through which you can filter in new opportunities, ideas, thoughts, situations and circumstances to help you get what you are seeking.

Journaling also helps you build a plan. You wouldn't try to build a house without a blueprint would you? Journaling helps you build a blueprint for your life. This will greatly improve the likelihood of you achieving it.

3. Journaling helps you strengthen your self-discipline

When you set time aside to write daily, whether in the morning, evening or mid-day, it will require self-discipline. You will need self-discipline to establish and maintain this habit, particularly if you have never used a journal before. By journaling daily, you will begin to achieve more and make more progress towards your goals. Hence your journaling habit can be a good example of what self-discipline is capable of accomplishing in your life.

4. Journaling can heal you psychologically and physically

Writing about your feelings has been shown through a series of studies to have healing properties. Pennebaker asked people who had experienced loss and trauma to do nothing else other than write about their feelings for 4 to 5 days, 20 minutes at a time. This minimalist use of writing proved to be a successful psychological intervention as it produced significant psychological and health benefits. Pennebaker says, "When we translate an experience into language we essentially make the experience graspable."[62]

Another study showed that one group of individuals who kept a journal about things they were grateful for, helped to increase their levels of determination, attention, enthusiasm and energy, compared to other groups in the experiment who journaled about things which annoyed them or reasons why they were better off than other people.[29]

5. The pen is more powerful than the keyboard

Research by Pam Mueller and Daniel Oppenheimer found that students who wrote their lecture notes out on paper learned more than those who typed notes on an electronic device.[59] Across three experiments, they got students to take notes in a classroom setting then tested them on their recall of factual details, conceptual understanding of the material and their ability to synthesize and generalize the information. Half the students took notes on a laptop and the other half took written notes.

In all three studies, the students who took the written notes outperformed the students who typed their notes. The writers had superior recollection and better memory of the material. They also had greater conceptual understanding of the material and were also more able to integrate and apply the information than the students who typed their notes.

Why the difference? The researchers suggest that you use different cognitive processing mechanisms when you take notes by hand, as opposed to using a laptop. Notes are slower and more cumbersome, and you have to be more selective with what you write in a lecture. You have to listen more intently, summarise more succinctly and process the information deeper. Writers have to force their brains into some "heavy lifting" due to the need to gain deeper comprehension and retention of the material.

For the group who typed their notes, they were able to take copious amounts, practically recording the lecture verbatim. This meant their minds entered a more mindless state requiring less deep processing of the material.

KEEPING A GOAL ACHIEVERS JOURNAL

I believe your primary mechanism for exposing yourself to your goals should be via the written method, and secondarily to use technology as a means of supplementing this. I will discuss the use of technology later in the Chapter.

I have designed The Goal Achievers Journal to help you imprint into your subconscious mind your highest and most valued goals. What's more the journal helps you to plan your next action steps, reflect on your progress, and assess your latest accomplishments and achievements. As such the journal is a key tool of change, which will radically shift the way you look at life and how you approach achieving what you desire most.

There are a few practical ways to get your own journal going.

1. Purchase a copy of **"The Goal Achievers Journal"** online. This is a 90 day journal, printed and bound. It also contains other sections useful for keeping track of your long term goals and for creating dream boards.

2. As a reader of this book, you have been given access to a free copy of the journal. You can download the journal, print it, and bind or file it. You can get a free copy from my site: www.davidbartontraining.com/freejournal.

3. Get an exercise book, and create your own journal.

Please be aware that I continually update and improve my journal, so the images shown here may be different from the journal you eventually receive, be that through download or purchase. However, the basic premise will always be the same. The Goal Achievers Journal has several key sections which contribute to the overall achievement of your goals. Each section has a particular use and should be filled in daily if possible.

Why bother keeping a journal?

1. You should keep a journal to program your subconscious mind with the details and particulars of what's important to you (your goals, dreams, and highest objectives).

2. The journal is meant to become an integrated part of your life and kept daily. The Goal Achievers Journal is a 90 day journal. Once completed, simply start a new one. If you miss a day or two it's not a disaster, just pick up where you left off as soon as possible. Remember you are sowing the seeds of change, and laying the foundations for what you want most in life. You can't expect to reap a harvest unless you first sow the seed.

3. By completing your journal daily, you will be sending very strong conscious messages to your mind which signal that attaining your goals are exceedingly important to you. By filling out your journal daily you are demonstrating your commitment to yourself which subsequently gets translated by the subconscious that these goals are important to you. You will therefore begin behaving in a more consistent manner with your beliefs.

4. Your daily habit of reflecting on your progress and achievements will send positive feedback messages to your subconscious, which will improve your mood and motivation. You will gain more self-confidence in your ability to get what you are aiming for.

5. As you write out your goals daily, you will be cognitively processing your goals at a deeper level. The daily act of writing out your goals will not only imprint the seriousness of attaining these goals onto your subconscious mind, it will also activate the power of your creative mind. You will start to see new ideas and solutions emerge. The how part of achieving your goals will begin to take shape and you will begin to realise the means by which you will attain your dreams.

6. As you work on your most important goals, you will need to decide on your next action step. Each and every day, you need to take some small measurable step in the direction of

your No 1 Goal. As you do this you will be constantly moving towards your destination, inch by inch.

7. In association with your No 1 Goal, you should also be working on several other goals which are important to you. By doing this you will create more balance in your life. Soon you will notice that you are attaining improvements in many other areas of your life you may have previously neglected.

How To Setup Your Goal Achievers Journal

The Goal Achievers Journal has been designed to maximise your exposure to your goals. Here are a few key sections which will maximise your exposure to your most important goals and which should be included in your journal.

Vision Board

The primary reason for your vision board is to place visual stimuli which represent your dreams, goals and aspirations before you on a daily basis. A picture is worth a thousand words, and your mind is built to process visual stimuli with more brain circuitry than for any of your other sensory inputs. The power of a vision board to shape your subconscious mind should not be underestimated. To maximise the use of your vision board, you should find pictures which represent what you want to achieve, own and be most in life. These might be pictures of where you want to go on holiday, the type of house you want to live in or the car you want to drive. It might also be pictures of the type of job you want, for instance if you want to be a doctor you can find pictures of doctors working in the kinds of places you desire to work in. Your images should also represent your most important values, such as images of you and your family enjoying life together. You should look at your vision board each day to feed your mind and spirit.

Long Term Goals

Your long term goals provide you with a big picture of what you want to achieve in life. They give you an aerial view of the terrain, so that you can plot a course to your destination. It is easier to notice the smaller steps you need to take when you have an idea of where you are heading. In the section entitled *long term goals*, think ahead, at least 5 years and describe what you want to have achieved in that time. Usually we overestimate what we can achieve in 1 year, but we generally underestimate what we can achieve in 5 years. So let your mind expand your horizons and dream big. You will be amazed at what you can accomplish in 5 years' time.

Short term Goals

Short term goals are the key to great achievement. They are essential because they give you a very specific target to focus your attention on, right now. They are also easily achieved in the short term because their demands are usually smaller. Achieving short term goals are similar to putting up scaffolding, because they help you climb higher and higher on your journey to the top. As you achieve each level you gain more and more confidence with each step. Each small success breeds more success. This journal is made up primarily of daily entries which represent your short term goals. Here is an example of how you can use the journal to achieve your most important goals.

Example of how to use your journal

Sarah wants to complete a PhD in English Literature at Harvard University. She applies and gets accepted. She plans on completing her degree in 3 years. She decides that this is her most important goal right now. So on 01/01/2016 she writes her No 1 Goal as, *"I have completed a PhD in English Literature on 31/12/2019."* She still wants to apply for a university scholarship, find a suitable thesis supervisor, find a flat to let, and a whole lot of other goals which she needs to achieve to succeed at her No 1 Goal.

Sub-goals by themselves might have several tasks associated. So for instance, Sarah's sub goal of applying for a university scholarship will entail several tasks such as filling in a scholarship application form, finding suitable references, making copies of supporting documentation, and posting the form to the correct address. All of these tasks are directly related to her sub-goal of applying for a scholarship. Taking all this information we can fill in the relevant sections of the journal like this:

Your No 1 Goal is broken down into several sub-goals

Your Sub-Goals are broken down into several supporting tasks.

The time scheduler is not meant to replace your diary, rather it supports your diary by helping you assign time to pursue your most important goals.

	My No 1 Goal
1	I have completed a PhD in English Literature on 31/12/2019
Sub-Goal No	**Sub Goals**
1	I have sent in a scholarship application by 30/03/2016
2	I have contacted 3 potential supervisors by 28/2/2016
3	Sarah continues to write in any of the other sub-goals she has to achieve...
4	
5	
6	
7	
8	

Sub-Goal No	**Today's Tasks**	**Done** ☑
1	Download scholarship application form from university website	☐
1	Read through application form and make a list of supporting documentation	☑
2	Read through departmental website and make note of potential supervisors to contact next week	☐
	Sarah lists other tasks she needs to complete for these and other sub-goals	☐
		☐

Time	Today's Schedule
5:00 am	
6:00 am	
7:00 am	
8:00 am	
9:00 am	Phone university office
10:00 am	
11:00 am	
12:00 pm	
1:00 pm	Make copies of supporting documents
2:00 pm	
3:00 pm	
4:00 pm	

Make Time Blocks in your schedule to work on these tasks

- As you complete your tasks, tick them off when they are done.
- Un-ticked tasks should be evaluated in terms of areas of procrastination or challenges faced.

Recently I Procrastinated On
I have not contacted a supervisor yet. I keep putting it off.

Today's Greatest Challenge
I am afraid of quitting my job and studying full time for 3 years.

As you notice areas you are procrastinating in, you might realise issues which are holding you back: Like fear of change, or the unknown.

The power of the Journal

The true power of The Goal Achievers Journal is experienced with the continual implementation of the process. As time progresses, Sarah will experience the achievement of many of her sub-goals. As she completes her sub-goals, they fall off the list and new ones enter on to it. Each time this occurs Sarah will find herself one step closer to the accomplishment of her No 1 Goal.

Today's Thoughts and Plans

You will ideally have a separate page in your journal for daily self-reflection and planning. Setting your daily goals are indeed essential to great achievement, but unless you plan to achieve those goals, you won't.

In the reflection and daily planning section of your daily journal you can process your thoughts, feelings and ideas with more depth. There are no rules here, you have carte blanche with whatever you want to write.

Some ideas are:

1. Aha moments and what your revelation was

2. New solutions to your problems

3. Your feelings about important issues

4. People you need to contact

In the Goal Achievers Journal I have included quotes and questions to help your reflective process and get the creative juices flowing. This will help you each day to better assess your values and beliefs and consider how they fit into the overall process of achieving your most important goals.

When your values and goals are not in alignment you will find yourself pursuing the wrong goals and end up with a hollow victory when you arrive at your destination. Each day you are presented with a new question to help you assess what's most important to you, to keep you on the road which will bring you the most value in life.

Here is an example of how you can set up this section of your journal.

Today's Thoughts and Plans

"To live a creative life, we must lose our fear of being wrong." *Joseph Pearce*

_____
_____
_____
_____
_____
_____
_____
_____
_____
_____
_____
_____
_____

At what time in your recent past have you felt most passionate and alive?

The true power of the journal is in its continual use. It is recommended to fill out the journal every day if possible. By doing so you will expose yourself to your most important goals with great regularity. The effect of this should not be underestimated. You will literally program your mind with what you want most out of life. As your thoughts are constantly directed towards your most important dreams and desires you will notice them begin to appear in your world. Not by magic, but by deliberate action which you will be taking to make your dreams come true. Your thoughts direct your actions, and when your thoughts are on your goals you will direct your actions to achieve them.

Ideas For More Constant Reminders

The importance of reminding yourself daily of your best goals can't be stated enough. Advertisers know how important it is to keep reminding us of their products and services; they have developed strategies to ensure their messages are constantly being beamed into our brains.

Likewise you can set up your environment where you are constantly reminded, or bombarded, by your goals.

One strategy to achieve this is to create signs containing statements of your goals and placing them conspicuously all around you. Some examples could include:

- Study wall
- Office wall
- Back of the bathroom door
- Back of the cover of your paper-based calendar (if you use one)
- On your car's steering wheel

- On your favourite mirror

- On the fridge door

- If you have a personal gym, place it on the roof, so you can see it when you are doing bench press.

- Create a desktop wallpaper containing your goals

- Your home screen in your mobile phone

- Billboard at the office

- Office corridors

- Company slogan

- Company website

- Periodic reminders in mass emails sent to staff

- On the edge of your monitor

- Engrave it on your frequently-used gadgets like your laptop, mobile phone or tablet computer

The main idea here is to place your goals where you will most likely see them, and so be reminded of what's important to you. The visual reminders will cause you to think of your goals and will activate the law of attraction, because what you think about most of the time will become your reality. What you focus your thoughts on most will begin to appear around you. What you give your attention to will manifest into your world. So maximise the opportunities to be reminded of your goals to maximise the power of your subconscious mind.

Supplement With Technology

As the Law of Attraction reminds us, we should expose ourselves regularly to our mission statement and goals so they are always in the forefront of our minds. Technology can be used to benefit us in this process.

One of the best ways to do this is to think like an advertiser.

The most effective advertisers place their messages in places where they know people frequently look. For example research shows that there are very specific "hot spots" on a web page where people look most of the time. Advertisers surreptitiously place adverts in these locations to gain maximum exposure for their messages. You can use the same thinking to generate ideas to constantly bombard yourself with your mission statement and goals.

Consider using some of the following techniques to automate your process:

1. **Automatic reminders.** You can program automatic reminders into Microsoft Outlook and Gmail for example to send you a daily email reminding you of your most important goals, mission statement, etc.

2. **Automatic notifications**. You can use mobile phone apps to send automatic notifications.

3. **Receive positive messages**. Subscribe to services that offer positive and inspiring daily messages.

4. **Google Alerts**. Google alerts is a useful tool which sends you daily links to articles and information about a particular subject you want Google to search for. You tell Google Alerts your keyword/s and it will do a daily search and email you the results daily. You can use this to search for information updates on topics related to your goals.

Using Mental Rehearsal

Mental rehearsal is a psychological technique you can use to program your brain with visual information by imprinting this information on the screen of your mind. Using mental imagery, you visualise a task before you attempt it physically. The technique has been promoted as a performance enhancing method for years. It has been researched in several experimental studies and shown to work. Top athletes, musicians, sales people and business people use it to enhance their performance.

You begin the process by having a clear idea of what you want to achieve. For example your goal might be to interact and communicate more freely with new people at a party. Once you are clear about your goal you construct a mini movie in your mind. You picture yourself interacting, laughing and chatting with many new people at a party. You see yourself enjoying contact with new people, not feeling self-conscious or shy. You notice that people are enjoying your company and having a good time in your presence. At the end of the movie you see yourself as having achieved your goal.

You play this scene on the screen of your mind several times per day. The more you do it the better the chances that your subconscious mind will believe it. The theory behind this strategy suggests that the mind and central nervous system cannot distinguish between actual and imagined memories. The brain simply records the event as actual experiences. When you eventually attempt the actual behaviour your mind already has mental experiences to refer to.

KEY POINTS TO REMEMBER

- To help you pursue and achieve your goals you should be using the inbuilt automaticity of your brain to your best advantage. Your brain has been created to help you develop habits and routines to drive your actions. These habits can be positive or negative – it's your choice. You can develop good success enhancing habits and program them into your subconscious. These habits produce actions which automatically pursue your goals.

- You can program your mind to filter into your awareness any input which is relevant to your goals. You can filter out irrelevant information and pay closer attention to people, places and situations which are directly relevant to you achieving your goals. To configure your filter, you need to have clarity of what it is you want. When you are clear about your goals, you can better program your filter.

- The Law of Attraction is based on the idea that you will draw into your life people, places, objects and situations which dominate your thoughts. This is based on the idea that your thoughts determine your actions. Your actions will generally be consistent with your dominant thoughts. The corollary of this is that if your thoughts are filled with the dreams, desires and goals you have for your life, your actions will be directed towards attaining them. You get what you think about most of the time; think about your goals and you will attain them.

- In general, journal writing has many benefits. More specifically, keeping a goal achievers journal will help you achieve your goals. By keeping a goal achievement journal daily, you will consistently and continuously sow the seeds of change into your mind. This powerful habit will place your most important objectives and priorities in the forefront of your mind on a daily basis, and associated with your daily next action step you will activate your goals and bring them to fulfilment.

- You should use technology to supplement your exposure to your goals as much as possible. Set automatic reminders, and visual cues to continuously sow the seed into your subconscious mind. Saturate your environment with images of what you hold most important, and let your mind be filled with positive thoughts of what it is you want to achieve most. Remember that thoughts become real when you give more attention to them.

CHAPTER 8

Persistence: Keep going in tough times

"A little more persistence, a little more effort, and what seemed hopeless failure may turn to glorious success."

Elbert Hubbard

How do you define persistence? Winston Churchill defined it well. He was a key figure from our recent past, who really understood what persistence truly meant, having himself endured several difficult situations and major events, one being the Second World War.

One day, much later in his life, Churchill was visiting his old preparatory school, and was asked what the secret was to his great success.

Churchill certainly was a great success, having been at Britain's helm during the Second World War and having steered Britain through what was one of the most trying times in the world's history. One such difficulty he endured, was the bombing of the city of London. For a full 3½ months, the Nazis dropped bombs on London without letting up.

It was during this time that Churchill delivered that inspiring speech,

"We shall go on to the end, we shall fight in France,
we shall fight on the seas and oceans,
we shall fight with growing confidence and growing
strength in the air, we shall defend our Island, whatever
the cost may be, we shall fight on the beaches,
we shall fight on the landing grounds,
we shall fight in the fields and in the streets,
we shall fight in the hills;
we shall never surrender . . . "

Back at the preparatory school, standing in front of the assembly, Churchill leans on his cane, and in his usual confident sturdy voice says, "I can summarise the lessons of my life in seven words: never give in; never, never give in."

So what is the secret of success?

If you are looking for the secret of success, it is as Churchill aptly said, "Never give in."

Many other great minds have echoed the same sentiment.

World Heavyweight boxing champion, James Corbett, once remarked, "You become a champion by fighting one more round. When things are tough, you fight one more round."

Likewise, Confucius said, "Our greatest glory is not in never falling, but in rising every time we fall."

To be a person of great persistence you need to build an iron clad attitude of never staying down, and getting back up again and again.

American football player and coach Vince Lombardi once said, "It's not whether you get knocked down, it's whether you get up."

A Japanese proverb iterates, "fall seven times, stand up eight."

The message is clear and simple: don't quit, don't give in, keep getting up, and never stay down.

If there is just one lesson you can take away from this Chapter, it is if you want to achieve great success in life and achieve your best self, never give up the dream, keep pushing forward, and never give in.

What Is The Best Predictor Of Success?

Many people want to know what the secret of success is.

Some believe the secret to great achievement is intelligence. Others believe it is talent. Still others think it is character, attractiveness, or family background. Still others consider it to be a personality dimension such as extroversion, disagreeableness or some other personality factor.

The truth is that none of these factors alone have been implicated in predicting success. Sure they contribute to it, but on their own they are weak. Recent scientific research has discovered that there is a trait which can predict success.

Findings from resent studies show that it is not intelligence, talent or confidence which can best predict achievement. The true secret to achieving your dreams is determined by your level of persistence, which has also become known as GRIT.

Calvin Coolidge once impeccably stated, "Nothing in this world can take the place of persistence. Talent will not: nothing is more common than unsuccessful men with talent. Genius will not; unrewarded genius is almost a proverb. Education will not: the world is full of educated derelicts. Persistence and determination alone are omnipotent."

So like it or not, if you want to attain greatness and achieve your richest dreams and desires you will need a healthy dose of persistence.

According to Angela Duckworth, one of the forerunners in this area of research, "Grit is passion and perseverance for very long-term goals. Grit is having stamina. Grit is sticking with your future, day in, day out, not just for the week, not just for the month, but for years, and working really hard to make that future a reality. Grit is living life like it's a marathon, not a sprint."[25]

Duckworth has conducted several studies in the context of exceptional performance and success. Specifically, she has explored cases where talent and intelligence (IQ) being equal has shown that some individuals just seem to accomplish more than others. Duckworth set out to find out why.

Duckworth developed the Grit Scale, which rates people on how much they agree with statements such as, "I finish whatever I begin," "I have overcome setbacks to conquer an important challenge," and reverse-scored statements such as, "My interests change from year to year."

She used this scale to assess adults aged over 25 who visited her website, www.authentichappiness.org, as well as to Ivy League undergraduates, West Point cadets and Scripps National Spelling Bee finalists.

Her results across 6 studies showed that individuals who showed more grit outranked their less gritty peers.

For example, persistent undergrads achieved higher grade point averages than their less persistent peers. Grittier West Point cadets were likelier to stay on after the first summer. And among the spelling-bee participants, "grittier" spellers out spelled their less tenacious competitors.[26]

Duckworth was surprised by one discovery though: Grit was not yoked to IQ. Her findings suggested that you don't need to be highly intelligent to achieve astonishing results. You don't have to be overly smart to do great things with your life.[2]

---

[2] You can read more about the lack of correlation between intelligence and success in Malcolm Gladwell's book Outliers.

The good news according to Duckworth is that you can learn to be grittier. In essence, you can learn to be more persistent.

Duckworth concluded, "If it's important for you to become one of the best people in your field, you are going to have to stick with it when it's hard," she says. "Grit may be as essential, as talent is, to high accomplishment."

Basically, high accomplishment requires great persistence.

Expect To Get Knocked Down

At this stage, I hope it has become apparent that persistence is firstly about stick-ability; the tenacity to keep getting up when you get knocked down. And to be clear, life will knock you down – this is a given.

Secondly, to achieve your highest goals through persistence you should *expect* to get knocked down. Don't expect an easy ride to glory, don't assume you will just glide into victory. You will have to fight for it.

You should assume setbacks, anticipate roadblocks and realise that you will have to regularly navigate obstacles and barriers. This is an unavoidable aspect of life and one you will become familiar with should you decide to go after your highest dreams and priorities. You will have to fortify your determination and strengthen your resolve.

As World Heavyweight boxing champion James Corbett said, "You become a champion by fighting one more round. When things are tough, you fight one more round."

To be persistent and fight one more round, means you must be willing and ready to take another pounding. You must be willing to get knocked down again, and again. You must be ready to experience more pain; to be punched in the face, and hit in the stomach.

So in a way, persistence invites trials and tribulation into our lives. It is no easy task to be persistent. You get knocked down, you fail, and you lose. This is what it means to persist. This may not be the picture you want to see, but it is the reality.

The great heavy weight champion of the world, Muhammad Ali, once said, "I never thought of losing, but now that it's happened, the only thing is to do it right. That's my obligation to all the people who believe in me. We all have to take defeats in life."

Ali accepted that to move on he needed to accept defeat. But he stood up again, he persisted, and this is the hallmark of a true success, of a true champion.

Churchill expected to get knocked down but refused to stay down. Two phrases from Churchill's address to the nation were, "we shall defend our Island, whatever the cost may be" and "we shall never surrender." Churchill showed clear intent that they were going to get up and fight to the bitter end, no matter the cost.

Surrender was not an option. Yet it might have been this very attitude of heart which won them the war. As B.C Forbes, the founder of Forbes magazine, who built a major publication during a The Major Depression once said, "History has demonstrated that the most notable winners usually encountered heart-breaking obstacles before they triumphed. They won because they refused to become discouraged by their defeats."

Likewise, Conrad Hilton, who built a mega chain of luxury hotels all over the globe said, "Success seems to be connected with action. Successful people keep moving. They make mistakes, but they don't quit."

Both research and personal experience has converged to pronounce an unwavering message; if you want to be truly successful, you need to have persistence. Never give up, never say die, is the secret to great success and achievement. It was 1000 years ago, and it still is today.

Pursue The Right Thing

Knowing that persistence is the key ingredient to achieve your grandest dreams is one thing, but you also need to show wisdom in choosing what you will persist on.

It is pointless to persist at something you are not passionate about. It is like what Steven Covey says about scrambling up the ladder of success only to find when you reach the top that you were leaning against the wrong wall.

Stephen Kellogg says it best, "It's better to be at the bottom of the ladder you want to climb than at the top of the one you don't."

It's a sad situation when you arrive at the place you have been aiming for, only to find it wasn't the place you wanted to be in the first place. It's a hollow victory to work hard, relentlessly overcoming barriers and obstructions, to later discover you made the trip for nothing. This is what happens when you are unclear about your values, dreams, beliefs, and passions.

What you choose to persist at is as equally important as being a person who reflects high levels of persistence. Peter Drucker says, "There is nothing so useless as doing efficiently, that which should not be done at all."

The sad truth is that we often get stuck in doing the wrong things, but don't have the courage to stop or get out. We may have sunk to much time, effort, money, or energy into the endeavour that we are unwilling to lose that which we have invested. This is a common problem which is known as the sunk cost fallacy.

The Sunk Cost Fallacy

Often when we make important decisions, we will sink time, money, effort and energy in to the process. Once paid these costs cannot be recovered. We see them as a type of investment, and usually we weigh this information heavily when we make our decision, even if the decision is the wrong one. Basically we are reluctant to lose our initial investment, which leads us to falling prey to the sunk cost fallacy.

Getting duped by the sunk cost fallacy is surprisingly common. Here are a few examples:

1. You continue eating all the food on your plate because you don't want to waste

This is particularly evident in a restaurant, where you are reluctant to waste food you are paying for. The greater the cost, the less likely you will be inclined to leave any food on your plate. So you persist and eat it all up.

Buffets are really bad for this. You pay one price and then you eat as much as you can manage. To get value for money, most people keep going up to the buffet to reload their plates. At the end of the meal they would have eaten far more than usual.

2. You continue to watch a movie which you are not enjoying because you already sunk 30 - 40 minutes into it

How do you feel about abandoning a TV series you have been watching for years because it has gotten predictable, boring and no longer grabs your attention?

What about that book you have been struggling to get into. Are you more inclined to put it down and get something more interesting, or just struggle through? Is there a difference if it's a library book or one you have bought.

If you go to the cinema, where you paid a fair price for the ticket, and the movie sucks, are you going to get up and walk out?

In all these cases we persist at doing something we might be better off ending. As you can see in these cases persistence has a negative effect.

3. You continue on a study program you are not interested in

I imagine this happens very frequently. People enrol in an undergraduate degree, or diploma course, to find that they are reluctant to bail out when they discover it's not their cup of tea.

It costs big money to go to university, so the sunk costs usually represent a sizeable amount. And the educational system is setup in a way that if you bail out before you complete the final paper, you leave with nothing. In this case you have nothing to show for your big student loan. Most people will persist and complete the program rather than get out now.

4. You continue investing in a bad relationship to avoid sunk costs

Let's face it your relationships probably represent your biggest cost of all.

If you don't believe me, look at the fortunes spent on resolving high profile divorce cases. Millions and millions of dollars get spent in courts annually dividing up resources between people whose relationships have dissolved.

People put huge investments into their relationships of time, money, and energy.

Before you say "I do" make sure the person is the right one for you. Don't base your decision on how much money you have spent wining and dining together.

To persist in a bad relationship due to the sunk cost fallacy is certainly bad advice.

What can you do about sunk costs?

Recognize that you fall victim to this logical fallacy. By being aware of this fallacy you will be more prepared to deal with it in the future. Usually some aspect of it creeps into your decision making processes, so look out for it the next time you have to make a decision.

Write out a pros and cons list. Delineate all the benefits of following a certain decision and list off all the negatives.

Ask yourself these questions:

1. Think about a recent significant purchase you made. Would you make the same purchase again? Why or why not?

2. Have a look in your wardrobe and dig out that old suit or dress. When did you last wear it? Why is it still in your wardrobe?

3. Are you in a relationship, work or study program purely because you want to avoid losing your investment of time and money in these areas? What opportunities have you lost due to these decisions?

4. Think of a recent major decision you made. Did you have sufficient information when you made your decision? Now that you are wiser would you have made the same decision again? What have you done about the situation you originally decided upon?

5. Do you need to prove yourself right based on previous decisions? Would you rather stay trapped in a bad situation than make a change? Is it more important to be right than to be happy?

Maintaining The Status Quo

We all like keeping the status quo (staying the same and not changing or adapting), it is a more comfortable and predictable way to live than the alternative. We are extremely good at persisting when it comes to maintaining the status quo.

Maintaining the status quo is something which is engrained deep within our psyche. It is what we are programmed to do. That is why our habits are so hard to break or change.

One factor which strengthens our resolve to maintaining the status quo is the manner in which we perceive loss. Many studies show that people are far more motivated to prevent loss than to obtain gain. [79]

This is known as loss aversion. Moreover, the psychological effect of loss is twice as powerful as the effect of gain. We tend to exaggerate the loss component and minimise the gain. What we gain by achieving our goal needs to be far greater than what we lose; much greater (and yes you do lose something in this exchange).

If your goal for instance is to lose weight, the change in your diet will most likely be perceived as a loss (possibly a big one). Hence, your goal of losing weight will have to provide you with twice the reward to overcome your feelings of loss. You will have to benefit twice as much if you hope to break the status quo.

That's why you should set big goals. Big goals push you way beyond your point of loss perception. They provide you with a reward that makes your loss seem infinitesimally small. The perceived gain from massive goals will effectively neutralise the psychological effects of loss that you will experience due to having to give up something important. As Michael Korda says, "One way to keep momentum going is to have constantly greater goals."

Bigger goals will produce bigger rewards which will have the potential to break through the inertia produced by the status quo. It can be hard to get the ball moving, particularly a big one, as the effort required is so much greater than the effort of just staying the same. Michelangelo once remarked, "The greater danger for most of us isn't that our aim is too high and miss it, but that it is too low and we reach it." Low aim is similar to maintaining the status quo and gets you nothing more than the same thing you have always gotten.

For some people, breaking the status quo is exceedingly difficult. Even when threatened with an imminent life or death situation, they make no effort to change. The problem is that their goals may not provide sufficient reward to overcome their perception of loss.

Goals need to be bigger, and more meaningful to activate motivation to change. If the reward is not big enough you will probably just maintain the status quo and keep doing what you have always done.

Persistence can work as much against us as it can for us. We can just as easily persist in following the wrong path as we can the right one. Once in a rut it is hard to break out. Any attempt to break out of a rut is met by resistance; mostly self-imposed resistance. Even when our actions and behaviours have negative consequences, we continue with them, because change is perceived as loss, a threat to our freedom, which we vehemently fight against.

Much of your success will depend on the path you find yourself on, the groove you find yourself in, or the routines and habits you have formed. In Chapter 9: Self-Discipline, we consider habits and routine in more detail, but for now the lesson is that you will persist at any habit you have developed, good or bad, and changing these aspects of your behaviour will come with resistance.

Persist At What You Good At, Delegate The Rest

Billionaire Richard Branson manages over 400 companies but still has plenty of time to spend on his private island and break crazy world records. He said in an interview with Inc. Magazine, "Early on in your career, find someone better than yourself to run the business on a day-to-day basis. Remove yourself, maybe even from the building, and from the nitty-gritty. That way, you're going to be able to see the bigger picture and think of new areas to go into."[63]

For Branson, doing the right thing is to step aside and let others run the day to day operations of his many companies. This leaves him to focus on what he is good at, doing the work he enjoys most, and which he is more able to persist at.

Branson is a visionary. He is a big picture thinker. This is his talent and his strength. He has done exceedingly well in life because he has focussed on his strengths and identified his weaknesses. He is in the enviable position to appoint others to do the work he is not equipped to do. These are the jobs others are able to do better than him.

When you delegate, you are admitting that you cannot do the whole enchilada, that you are not good at everything, that you have limitations. This is hard for some people. They are perfectionists and insist that they are the only ones who can do the job right. But it comes at a cost. It takes your mind off your No 1 Goal. It steals your time and removes your focus.

Some people may complain and say that he is Richard Branson, so he has the luxury to focus on his most important goals, because he has other people running the day to day operations. But maybe this is like saying the apple came before the tree. Personally I think Richard Branson is in this enviable position, because once upon a time he focused on his most important goals and that got him into a position to employ others to run his businesses. He built the tree that produced the apples first.

Granted, for many people the pursuit of their No 1 Goal will come at a cost. They won't have the luxury to employ others to run their businesses, not at first. But in time the situation will begin to change, and they will discover more opportunities to invest time and energy into, until one day like Branson, they can spend all their important time doing the things which produce the biggest reward for them.

Stop Making Excuses

The great heavy weight boxer of the world, Muhammad Ali, once said, "When a man says I cannot, he has made a suggestion to himself. He has weakened his power of accomplishing that which otherwise would have been accomplished."

What limiting beliefs do you have? What excuses have you nurtured?

Our excuses can get in the way of our persistence. They offer a rationale for why we should quit. When we get knocked back our excuses give us a reason to stay down. Entrepreneur and motivational speaker Jim Rohn said, "If you really want to do something, you'll find a way. If you don't, you'll find an *excuse*."

Here are some excuses people make to hinder their stick-ability and grit:

1. **I have failed before, I will fail again:** It's not failing that you should fear, it's not trying that's the real enemy. Bruce Lee said, "Don't fear failure. — Not failure, but low aim, is the crime. In great attempts it is glorious even to fail."

2. **It's impossible:** If someone else has done it, then it is possible. Success is not reserved for a select few. Granted some things may come down to physical attributes and

genes, but for the most part, what is possible for one person is possible for another.

3. **I am too old to change:** People of all ages have achieved astounding feats. It is never too late. People in their 80's have climbed Everest, and 90 year olds have run marathons. Most millionaires are made after the age of 55. Don't limit your beliefs by your age.

4. **I don't know how to do it:** If you don't know how to do it, learn how. We live in the information age. For instance, nowadays there are online videos showing you how to do all sorts of things. There are millions of eBooks instantly available for download, on practically every subject imaginable. It does not come down to IQ it comes down to a willingness to learn.

Excuses will keep you down, they will give you reasons to bail out and throw in the towel. Persistence is about getting up when you are knocked down, never giving up and always trying one more time. Excuses are your enemy, while persistence is your ally. When the going gets tough, people with excuses throw in the towel and give themselves good reasons for doing so.

Some individuals have plenty of excuses to quit, while others seem to have many reasons to press on. Think of Thomas Edison, who is presumed to have tried 1,000 times to perfect the light bulb. Light bulbs may look simple, but they are surprisingly complicated devices. For one, the older type of bulbs which used an element, had to withstand the heat produced by the current flowing through it rather than burn out. Imagine all the different materials Edison would have had to trial before he found the best conductor. Most people would give up after a few attempts, but he didn't seem to have a quit button. The reward simply outweighed the costs. He could light up the world, or leave it to glow in candle light.

Make It Hard To Quit

There is an old story about a Spanish conquistador "conqueror" named Hernan Cortez who in 1519 made a life changing decision which can teach us all a useful lesson about never giving up.

During that year he sailed a fleet of 11 Ships from Spain to South America, and when he arrived, realised that occupying the land was going to come at a cost. The local natives were not about to relinquish possession of their land, and were ready to put up a fight (as you do). His men were tired, malnourished and demotivated. They had just endured a long arduous trip across the oceans, and were in no shape to do battle.

Cortez realised this dilemma, but circumstances prevented them turning back. He was stuck between the proverbial rock and a hard place. When he arrived, he sent all his troops on to the beach, and unbeknownst to them, proceeded to set all the ships on fire. He lit up the sky and burnt the vessels to a crisp.

With no way to retreat, Cortez figured his troops would have to get motivated to fight, or die. And they did. His troops gathered up their flailing courage, strength and motivation, and put up the biggest fight of their lives. They gained victory over the natives and proceeded to claim the land that is now known as Mexico.

For Cortez's men, retreat was not an option – their ships were ablaze. The message signalled by burning ships motivated Cortez's' troops to take up arms, but at the same time it sent shivers of fear down the spines of the natives.

The sight of burning ships may have sent an unequivocal message to the natives that these invaders were here to do business. It was signalling their intent loud and clear.

One message is clear from this story. If you truly want to achieve your goals, you need to remove all option of retreat. You need to send yourself a clear, unequivocal message that you mean business. For example:

- What message have you sent yourself that you mean business attaining your No 1 Goal?

- What message have you sent your family, friends and neighbours that you intend to pursue and obtain your No 1 Goal?

- If you are in business, what message have you sent your competitors that you intend to do battle on the economic front?

- If you are in school, university or college, what message have you sent your teachers, fellow students and parents that you intend to persist and succeed no matter the cost?

The message you send, signals intent!

It signals your motivation to succeed. It demonstrates your willingness to do what it takes to win.

What's more, the quality of this message will predict the level of your success.

As Napoleon Hill says regarding the prediction of someone's future. You simply have to ask him one simple question: "What is your one definite purpose for your life – and what plans have you made to attract it?"

Most people say, "I would like to earn a good living and be as successful as I can." This may appear to be a practical answer, but if you dig a little deeper you will find the opposite. This answer shows very little *intent*. It signals very little motivation. Hill says it is the words of a drifter who will not go on to achieve anything of significance in life, other than gaining the odd left over from truly successful people.[41]

Your message of intent to yourself and others needs to be clear and deliberate, not vague and indecisive.

No Retreat, No Surrender

You can tell someone who is serious about achieving their goals – they make it hard to quit and difficult to fail.

For instance consider an individual who is serious about losing weight. They clear out their fridge, pantry, and shelves of food which do not contribute to the fulfilment of their goals. They make it more difficult to give in to temptation.

When you make it hard for yourself to retreat you show commitment. You prove to yourself and everyone around you that you mean business, that your goals are not just pie in the sky. That they are important to you!

Sophocles once said, "Fortune is not on the side of the faint hearted." To achieve your loftiest goals will require a spirit of boldness and unflinching resolve. You may have to take extreme measures, and do the things you never imagined possible.

For example, if you are a big spender and have a goal to save a certain amount of money, setup a fixed term call account and make automatic payments into that account on a fixed schedule. Set the maturity date to a date when you need the money and no sooner.

If you have to study for your exams, but can't seem to stay away from the video games, remove the console and TV from the premises, and get someone to hold them with strict instructions not to give you access until your exams are over.

Like Cortez, you may need to find a way to block your retreat. Granted you may not have to go to the extremes he went to, but the principle is the same; to achieve your goals you have to close down the avenues which aid withdrawal and escape.

Do You Have A Burning Desire

To succeed at your loftiest and grandest goals you need to have a burning desire to win. Napoleon Hill says, "Every person who wins in any undertaking must be willing to cut all sources of retreat. Only by doing so can one be sure of maintaining that state of mind known as a burning desire to win - essential to success."

Hill says, "There is one quality which one must possess to win, and that is **definiteness of purpose**, the knowledge of what one wants, and a burning desire to possess it."

At this stage, if you have completed the exercises in the Chapters, you will have gained more knowledge of what it is you want. You will have uncovered your No 1 Goal and laid out plans to achieve it.

By using *The Goal Achievers Journal,* you will have started the process of imprinting your goals into your subconscious mind.

You may have even achieved several sub-goals by now, as you begin to align your actions with your dominant thoughts. In time your burning desire will elevate you to new levels, probably beyond what you or those closest to you ever imagined possible. Joseph Wirthlin says, "Desire, burning desire, is basic to achieving anything beyond the ordinary."

Having a clear purpose, and a burning desire to achieve it, will no doubt place you in the ranks of those who achieve goals way beyond the ordinary.

Persistence is about stick ability, it's about getting knocked down time and time again and yet rising up once more. Persistence is about never giving up, never throwing in the towel. When you link persistent action to your highest goals you have a formulae for success. You have a path to victory. You have a grip on the life you truly desire.

In closing, Philip Stanhope, 4th Earl of Chesterfield says it well, "Persist and persevere, and you will find most things that are attainable, possible."

KEY POINTS TO REMEMBER

- Persistence is having the tenacity or doggedness of purpose, to keep rising in the face of defeat. Persistent people get knocked down time and again, and yet they keep getting up. Persistent people have tremendous stick ability when it comes to achieving their grandest and loftiest goals. Like everybody else, they get knocked down, they fail, they lose, but they rise and try again.

- Researchers have discovered that persistence (a.k.a. grit) is one of the key traits which can predict success for long term goals. Intelligence, talent, attractiveness, extroversion and education are some factors which contribute to success, however, it is persistence which comes out on top. You can be a genius, and still fail miserably at achieving your goals. When it comes to great achievement, persistence is more valuable than genius.

- Persistence is no walk in the park. It will invite trials, pain and discomfort into your life. A persistent boxer will be hit in the face and punched in the stomach far more than one who stays down. When the going gets tough the tough certainly do get going, but their journey will not be void of hardship and difficulty. To persist you will have to endure a certain level of suffering.

- Though persistence is an excellent trait to nurture and develop it can work against you as much as for you. You need to show wisdom in deciding what you will persist on. It is pointless persisting at something you should have never been doing to begin with. Once again this highlights the importance of uncovering your No 1 Goal and gaining clarity about what you truly desire in life. Without this knowledge you may waste many years pursuing the wrong dream.

- The sunk cost fallacy can keep you stuck in a rut, reluctant to give up what you have previously invested in a bad past decision. We often get duped into sticking with bad decisions because of fear of losing our investments of time, money or energy. Usually it is better to cut your losses in favour of pursuing the goals and objectives you truly desire.

- Another way persistence works against us, is through our tendency to maintain the status quo. Much of this tendency occurs due to the effect of loss aversion, where we are more attuned to what we will lose rather than what we will gain. This highlights the need for big goals, because only big audacious goals, can provide sufficient reward to overcome our perception of loss.

- We should make it hard to quit, and close off as many escape routes as possible, to prevent us backing out from our goals. Like Cortez, we need to develop the iron clad attitude of no retreat, no surrender and burn our ships to prevent us running away.

CHAPTER 9

Self-Discipline: The power of self-control

"I think self-discipline is something, it's like a muscle. The more you exercise it, the stronger it gets."

Daniel Goldstein

In this Chapter we will be exploring one of the most important factors necessary for achieving your best self. If you want to take charge of your life and achieve your dreams, you will need a good dose of self-discipline. It is a key cog in the engine which drives your personal achievement. No one has ever achieved anything of worth without this key quality.

You need self-discipline to develop other success-enhancing behaviours, and habits like persistence, goal setting, goal planning and breaking procrastination.

What Are Your Barriers And Obstacles

In Chapter 5 you read about a planning process and hopefully you will have spent some time taking stock of some of the obstacles and barriers you might face on your journey to achieving your No 1 Goal. Now might be a good opportunity to review the barriers, challenges and obstacles you previously considered to be the most important obstructions to you reaching your highest goals. These obstructions will probably require self-discipline to overcome.

WHAT IS SELF-DISCIPLINE?

Self-discipline is having restraint, exercising self-control, having self-mastery, and exercising will power. Self-disciplined people have the ability to turn down the need for immediate pleasure and instant gratification, in favour of achieving their highest goals, objectives and priorities. It is having the power to take control over your emotions, impulses and actions. You cannot hope to succeed until your highest priorities, goals and objectives have taken their rightful place in your life. For this to happen requires self-discipline.

This is not an innate skill. We are not born with large wads of self-discipline. We learn this as we grow up. Some people learn it better than others.

In the same family you will find children with different levels of self-discipline. Their differences can be so stark you wonder how it's possible they grew up under the same roof. For instance, in the same household, some children keep their room clean without much nagging from their parents, whilst others need constant reminders and threats to get them moving.

Small children in particular struggle with self-discipline, or at least the ability to put off immediate gratification. There is a famous marshmallow experiment where four-year-old children were seated in a room with a marshmallow placed in front of them.[58] They were told that if they waited 15 minutes without eating the marshmallow, they would receive another one; doubling their take. Sounds like a good deal, doesn't it? But most children struggled with this and ate the marshmallow before the 15 minutes were up.

There were some children who had the self-control to wait, and they were rewarded with double the loot. These same children were also found to grow up achieving better grades at school and having healthier relationships. The lesson here is that when you have the ability to withstand initial gratification you will achieve greater success in the future.

There are two lessons we can take from this experiment. Firstly, self-discipline is not innate. We have to learn and develop it. We are not born abounding with high levels of self-discipline and self-control.

Self-discipline is like a muscle which you must flex regularly to make it grow. If you push weights, to get bigger and stronger you must keep adding more and more weight to your workouts. Your muscles will have to grow to cope with the extra demands. At first you will struggle to push the heavier weight, but in time you will find it easier to move it as your muscles grow bigger and stronger.

The same is true of self-discipline. It is harder to do in the beginning, but soon you will find your self-discipline muscle getting bigger and stronger. You will achieve your goals faster and easier. You will also be able to achieve bigger, more audacious goals because you have more self-discipline. The self-discipline you will require will be in direct proportion to the size of your goal. Big goals require big self-discipline.

It is not by coincidence that most of the greatest successes in the world are also people with high levels of self-disciple.

Secondly, the marshmallow experiment teaches us that people who have more self-discipline, achieve more in life. They get bigger rewards and end up with double the take home pay, the bigger house, the nicer car, the better job. Developing greater self-discipline will help you get more of the life you want.

Another study examined 36 different personality traits in children, and found only one factor to be positively correlated with college GPA (Grade Point Average). That factor was willpower. Children who had more willpower attained better grades and academic performance. Henry Van once remarked, "The strength of your life is measured by the strength of your will."

Still other studies show that people with high levels of self-control and self-discipline are more emotionally stable, are less depressed, better at dealing with anger and anxiety, and are less prone to alcohol and drug abuse. They have more stable marriages and make for better bosses.

Studies have shown that in the same family, siblings with more self-control fared better in life than their less self-controlled brothers and sisters.

So why learn to be more self-disciplined? One of the main reasons for learning more self-discipline is that it enables you to accomplish your long term goals. Self-discipline can help make your dreams come true sooner than later.

But gaining more self-discipline will not come easy. There are several reasons why people lack this important quality to begin with. After all, if it were easy everybody would be doing it!

Why People Lack Self-Discipline

One of the primary reasons people lack self-discipline is that they never placed much importance in developing it in the first place. If you grew up in a home which placed little value on self-discipline, then you may end up not placing much value on self-discipline later in life. Take a moment and think about your upbringing:

1. What were your families' attitudes to self-discipline?

2. Did your family members model good or bad self-disciplined behaviour?

3. What did you come to believe about the value of self-discipline?

People erroneously see self-disciple as a negative construct which is based solely on pain and discomfort. Though to a degree, developing self-discipline can be uncomfortable and cause some pain, the results are far more positive than negative. Self-discipline will help you achieve your life's dreams and get you more of what you richly desire. Pain and discomfort will be a minor inconvenience compared to the reward you will receive.

Another reason people lack self-discipline is that they interpret failure as a sign to give up. If you have the mind-set that failure signals the end, then you will fail to persist, and you will not need much self-discipline to try again. In those times when you try and fail, like we all do, you can just give up and throw in the towel. This is not the same as using failure to help you succeed. When you use failure as a resource for information on how not to do the same thing twice, you give yourself an excuse to try again, but this time using a different approach. This requires self-discipline and persistence.

For some people their lack of self-discipline is a function of their inability to withstand temptation and exercise resistance. If you easily give in to temptation you develop weak habits and mental frameworks. This makes you susceptible to the smallest enticements. All day long we are tempted to take the path of least resistance. Temptations steer us off course and wastes precious time and energy on fruitless activities.

Lastly, many people fail to develop self-discipline because they have no clear goals. When you have no clear goals, no purpose and no direction, you will have low motivation to exercise self-discipline. Just drifting from day to day with no purpose, nothing to achieve, nothing to gain, requires little self-discipline. There is not much self-discipline needed to accomplish going nowhere!

Lack of self-discipline may be the result of several factors such as:

- Family upbringing and values

- Having no clear goals and low aims

- An intolerance for discomfort

- Fear that developing self-discipline will cause you pain

- Easily giving in to temptations

To be a goal achiever will necessitate a change in this perception.

I read an interesting story about Gary Player, one of the most successful international golf players of all time.[86] He had lost count of how many times spectators said to him, "I'd give anything if I could hit a golf ball like you." Player figured that spectators would quickly change their minds if they knew what it took to hit the ball like he did.

After one particularly gruelling day on a links course, he finally couldn't resist correcting the person, "No, you wouldn't," he said.

Player continued, "You would give anything to hit a golf ball like me, if it were easy!"

Player then listed off all the things one would have to do in order to achieve his level of play: "You've got to get up at five o'clock in the morning, go out and hit a thousand golf balls, then walk up to the club house to put a bandage on your hand where it started bleeding, then go back and hit another thousand balls. That's what it takes to hit a golf ball like me."

Is developing self-discipline going to be easy? I think not. Like Gary Player you will have to face tedium, boredom, pain, and blood, sweat and tears. But is it worth it? Certainly! Like Player you too can rise in the ranks of greatness and become one of the best in the world at whatever it is you desire to do with your life.

Another professional golfer, Chi Chi Rodriguez, put it this way. He said, "Preparation through steady practice is the only honest avenue to achieving your potential."

But the world we live in is averse to self-discipline. People have become more accustomed to the comforts of modern day life. As the need for comfort increases so the desire to develop self-discipline has been relegated to the ash heap.

Surely living a comfortable life should be high on our list of goals, but it should never come at the cost of our health, fitness, relationships, faith, or anything else we hold important.

The Bible says, "Watch and pray so that you will not fall into temptation. The spirit is willing, but the flesh is weak (Matthew 26:41, NLT)". This is a very powerful scripture, because we are all prone to give in to our fleshly desires which impedes our path, and blocks us from our most important goals.

For many people the need to satisfy the desires of the flesh becomes the all-important quest of their lives, at the cost of sacrificing the chance of having a far greater and rewarding existence.

It Takes Self-Discipline To Develop Good Habits

Your success can only rise to the level of your weakest habit. In the past it was widely speculated that it took 21 days to develop a new habit. [28] Newer research shows that you can develop a new habit in anywhere from 18 – 254 days, with the average time being around 66 days.[49] It all depends on the type of habit you are trying to build.

But why do you want to develop new habits in the first place? Habits automate your behaviour, which allows you to achieve your goals faster. Octavia Butler, in an essay for aspiring writers, says, "First forget inspiration. Habit is more dependable. Habit will sustain you, whether you're inspired or not.... Habit is persistence in practice."

Charles Duhigg, author of *The power of habit: Why we do what we do in life and business*,[27] breaks down a habit into three key elements: cue, action, reward.

The presentation of the stimulus is the cue; the sight of the chocolate cake, the smell of roasted coffee beans, the sight of a Bull Mastiff, waking up in the morning, all cause you to experience a certain type of response.

The response may be to salivate at the presentation of cake or coffee, a tensing of the muscles at the sight of a Bull Mastiff, or brushing your teeth as soon as you get up in the morning. All of these responses are automatic and require no conscious effort. They occur in fractions of a second. You experience the cue and you produce the outcome; salivate, tense, brush teeth. Why do you do this?

Because you were rewarded in the past for taking similar actions; chocolate cakes taste good, coffee is an enjoyable hot beverage, and brushing teeth produces fresh breath and less cavities.

In many cases it can take as little as a single pairing of all three elements to establish an automatic behaviour. Usually you are scarcely aware that you have developed a new automatic response.

However, the next time you face the same or similar cue your response will be faster, because it has now become more automated and entrenched.

Of course, habits can be good or bad. They can either enhance our lives, or diminish them. They can either promote good health, or kill us faster. They can help us move towards, or away, from our goals. They can help us get started, or just stay sitting on the couch.

To pursue a more fulfilling and meaningful life, you want to develop more good habits and reduce the number of bad habits you have.

Your habits hold one of the most important keys to your success. Developing as many good habits as possible will help you get the life you want sooner than later.

In the next section are examples of habits successful people have developed which they practice daily, and which have helped them achieve their highest goals.

You can develop these habits too. If you want to achieve your best self, it pays to have good habits like these:

1. To achieve your best self, rise earlier in the morning. Get a head start on your day, before the rest of the world has woken up. To achieve your best self, develop mind over mattress. Don't let sleep dominate your life, rather sleep to live than live to sleep. Use the extra time to plan each day with purpose and action.

2. To achieve your best self, read for a minimum of 30-60 minutes daily to develop and expand your mind. Keep learning. Robin Sharma says, "To double your rate of earning you should triple your rate of learning."

3. To achieve your best self, re-write your major goals daily. Constantly remind yourself of your highest goals. Keep programming your subconscious mind with what you want and what is most important to you.

4. To achieve your best self, visualise your goals at every occasion. Paste pictures in your journal, on your walls, on your desktop screen and anywhere else which can prompt you and remind you of where you are heading.

5. To achieve your best self, prioritise your daily tasks. Don't leave your day to chance. Make time for your No 1 Goals so that you can continuously work on them.

6. To achieve your best self, document your daily thoughts, insights and ideas. Appreciate the value of self-reflection. Capture your insights on paper, computer, voice recorder, even paper towels, or toilet paper, to save your ideas from being lost. To achieve your best self, evaluate your day before you go to sleep at night.

7. To achieve your best self, constantly look for a problem to solve. Understand that to be successful in life you need to provide solutions for as many people as you can. While the average person is busy avoiding problems, top achievers accrue problems. Why? Because they know that every problem is an opportunity. They realise that they can have everything they desire if they help enough people solve their problems. To achieve your best self, constantly look for problems to solve, because you know a problem solved is a reward gained.

8. To achieve your best self, don't see failure as negative. View failure as a step towards your greatest success. Theodore Roosevelt said it clearly, "Far better is it to dare mighty things, to win glorious triumphs, even though checkered by failure... than to rank with those poor spirits who neither enjoy nor suffer much, because they live in a grey twilight that knows not victory nor defeat".

9. To achieve your best self, take more risks and step outside of your comfort zones. Don't be a person of convention. You don't need the approval of others. To a large degree, people who achieve their best self, are disagreeable. They are willing to stand up for what they believe, and are not swept away in the tide of mass approval.

10. To achieve your best self, develop relationships with smart, positive people who can help you grow. Don't hang around with turkeys if you want to soar with eagles. Negative people only bring you down; avoid them at all costs.

11. To achieve your best self, develop the mental capacity to think big and set audacious goals. Don't be afraid to dream big dreams, and set your sights on achieving things no one else has ever dreamed of. People who achieve their best self are the great shakers and movers of our time.

12. To achieve your best self, don't procrastinate but get down to taking action on your most important priorities today. Know what you want, and go out and get it. When you have a passion for what you do, you won't need much motivation to get yourself out of bed in the morning. You will have a burning desire to get moving each day to accomplish your dreams.

13. To achieve your best self, develop a deep respect for time. Realise that time is a limited resource which is rapidly running out. When you have an appreciation of each minute you have been graced with, you won't waste it floundering on unimportant and irrelevant activities. What's more you will respect other people's time like your own. You never intentionally arrive late to meetings, and always keep your commitments.

14. To achieve your best self, recognize that when you get knocked down, you will get straight back up again. Keep trying and never give up. Live like the Japanese proverb suggests "Get knocked down 7 times, stand up 8." To achieve your best self, go to the bitter end to achieve your goals. Be fearless and relentless in your quest for success.

15. To achieve your best self, take good care of your health and body. Exercise your body 3 to 5 times per week, for at least 45 minutes at a time. Understand the value of having a healthy body and a healthy mind. Experience the positive benefits of being fit, having more energy, improving your focus and increasing your willpower.

These are some of the habits developed by successful people. It takes self-discipline to develop these habits, but once gained, the habits will assist you in achieving your highest dreams and objectives.

This is one of the key uses of self-discipline; to program your subconscious with success enhancing habits. Whatever you feed into your life will determine the person you will become, and will define the level to which you will rise. It all depends on what you choose to feed your mind and spirit with – garbage in, garbage out.

The next story aptly illustrates this concept:

One day an old Cherokee Warrior was out walking in the forest with his grandson.

Turning to the young boy, he said, "There is a battle raging inside of me. It is an awful battle between two wolves. One is evil - he is filled with rage, greed, grief, guilt, gluttony, conceit, self-pity, blame, bitterness, weakness, deceit, dishonesty, pride, superiority, and ego.

The other wolf is good - he is joy, peace, love, hope, calmness, humility, thoughtfulness, compassion, understanding, kindness, truth, concern, and faith.

But the same fight is raging inside of you too, and inside every other person."

The grandson thought about it for a minute and then asked his grandfather, "Which wolf will win?"

The old Cherokee simply replied, "The one you feed."

The wolf you feed will determine your habits, and your habits will determine your life's outcome.

Establish Daily Routines

It is not surprising to learn that many successful people believe that much of their success has occurred due to the routines they established earlier on in their lives.

For instance, Mischa Elman, one of the greatest violinists of the twentieth century, was walking through the streets of New York City one afternoon when a tourist approached him. "Excuse me, sir," the stranger began, "could you tell me how to get to Carnegie Hall?" Elman sighed deeply and replied, "Practice, practice, practice."

Behind the humour in this story there is some truth; the people who get to perform in Carnegie Hall are the ones who have practiced, practiced and then practiced some more! Carnegie Hall represents a life of self-discipline. It exemplifies thousands of hours of dedicated, intentional practice.

For one man, Carnegie Hall is the attainment of his highest goals, for another it represents a place to spectate. For one man Carnegie Hall represents the achievement of his best self, for another man it is mere entertainment.

But we all have our Carnegie Hall's; the place we richly desire to get to. What is your Carnegie Hall? Are you willing to practice, practice, and practice, to get there?

Stephen King is another individual who learnt the power of establishing success enhancing routines. He is undoubtedly one of the most prolific writers of our time. In his daily routine, he writes 2000 words first and foremost before heading off to do other things. But 2000 words come first. King says, "Amateurs sit and wait for inspiration, the rest of us just get up and go to work."

Jerry Seinfeld is another good example of someone who understands the power of routine. During his days as a touring comic, Seinfeld established a routine which helped him achieve huge success. To motivate himself to write new material every day, he would put a big X over every single day he wrote. His small chain of X's grew longer as the weeks rolled on. He loved the positive benefits of producing new, fresh and interesting content for his acts, and became reluctant to break the chain.

Tiger Woods is undoubtedly one of the greatest golfers who has ever lived, and undeniably one of the hardest working athletes. Woods is a highly competitive and driven athlete, whose sole intention when playing in any competition is to win. He never plays to lose; losing has no place in his life.

Woods has developed daily practice schedules which would send most people running for cover. Here is an example of a daily schedule (source: http://www.businessinsider.com.au)

6:30 a.m. - One hour of cardio. Choice between endurance runs, sprints or biking.

7:30 a.m. - One hour of lower weight training. 60-70 per cent of normal lifting weight, high reps and multiple sets.

8:30 a.m. - High protein/low-fat breakfast. Typically includes egg-white omelette with vegetables.

9:00 a.m. - Two hours on the golf course. Hit on the range and work on swing.

11:00 a.m. - Practice putting for 30 minutes to an hour.

Noon - Play nine holes.

1:30 p.m. - High protein/low-fat lunch. Typically includes grilled chicken or fish, salad and vegetables.

2:00 p.m. - Three-to-four hours on the golf course. Work on swing, short game and occasionally play another nine holes.

6:30 p.m. - 30 minutes of upper weight training. High reps.

7:00 p.m. - Dinner and rest.

When you look at these big names, it is often easier to think that they got there by luck or by just being in the right place at the right time. Few people peer a little deeper to note the incredible self-discipline and sacrifice these individuals had to make, and the routines they had to establish to drive their great success.

Ways To Develop More Self-Discipline

Successful people have long known that having self-discipline is one of the key ingredients to achieving their best self. They have learned to leverage self-discipline by developing a number of good habits which help them push through the barriers they encounter along the road.

Theodore Roosevelt said, "With self-discipline most anything is possible." Likewise, Jim Rohm claimed "Discipline is the bridge between goals and accomplishment."

We have already established that big goals require big self-discipline, so it's no surprise that people like Tiger Woods and Steven King are people who exercise very high levels of self-discipline. Their levels of self-discipline would undoubtedly make many people shake in fear. But like these great achievers, you too can be great if you are willing to exercise the self-discipline you need to achieve your most highest and grandest goals.

In the next section I will present you with several ways you can use to develop more self-discipline.

Discipline the tongue

I have met several crass, rude and impudent people who have little control on their tongues. They defend their lack of self-control over their verbiage with an inane excuse like "what you see is what you get." This is meant to suggest that somehow, their vulgarity is excusable through their transparency.

Their words are more a reflection of what is on the inside of them. The Apostle James says, "The tongue also is a fire, a world of evil among the parts of the body. It corrupts the whole body, sets the whole course of one's life on fire, and is itself set on fire by hell (James 3:6:NIV)."

The truth is, what you say and express through your words have powerful implications on your life. Words have power, and carry meaningful consequences to the one who expresses them. Socrates shares a useful filter through which you can pass your words before expressing them to the world. I call it the GUT test and this is how you can apply it:

In ancient Greece, Socrates was known as a very wise and knowledgeable man. On one sunny day an acquaintance of his came over to him and began a conversation.

"Socrates", the man said, "You won't believe what I just heard about one of your friends."

Socrates looked up slowly, thought for a moment and then said, "Hold on a minute! Before you tell me anything about my friend, I want you to pass a little test. It is called the GUT test."

"GUT test?" said the man.

"That's correct," continued Socrates. "Before you tell me anything good or bad about my friend, it might be a good idea to first filter it through the GUT test. It is a triple filter test you see. The first filter is that of Goodness."

"What you want to tell me, is it something Good about my friend?"

"Good?" said the man, "Oh no, on the contrary…"

At this point Socrates interjects, "Okay, so it's not something good about my fiend. Now let's consider the second filter of the GUT test. Is what you are about to tell me something Useful about him?"

"Useful? Oh no not at all, but ..."

"Okay", said Socrates, interjecting once more, "So what you are about to tell me is neither good nor useful. But we have one more filter to go, so you might still past the test. Have you made absolutely sure that the information you want to pass on is True about him?"

"True? Well you see I only just heard about it and ..."

Cutting in for the last time Socrates summarises the conversation, "So what you want to tell me is not good, useful and you are not sure it is true. So exactly why do you want to tell me this at all?"

The lesson here is that the next time you want to pass on some information about another person, first weigh the information using the GUT test. If it fails the test, discard it and move on. Don't fill your mind and that of others with garbage.

Likewise the Apostle Paul says, "Finally, brothers and sisters, whatever is true, whatever is noble, whatever is right, whatever is pure, whatever is lovely, whatever is admirable--if anything is excellent or praiseworthy--think about such things (Philippians 4:8:NIV)."

Paul is admonishing us to keep our minds out of the gutter and on our most valuable and highest priorities and objectives. The message here is to guard your tongue. For some people this will be excessively difficult as they will require a huge amount of self-discipline to take control of this uncontrolled fire. Instead of spouting profanities and spreading unfounded gossip they will have to harness the tongue and keep it silent. But learning to do this, will greatly increase your level of self-discipline.

Develop Mental Toughness

For many people developing more self-discipline will come down to developing more mental toughness.

When I was young I figured this out when I did my 1 year compulsory military service in the South African Army.

During basic training, which lasts typically 3 – 6 months, new recruits are regularly subjected to corporal punishment, usually for the slightest infraction. Officers would pull up the entire unit on the smallest infringement. These would include slight blemishes in ironing, imperfect boot polishing, being slightly unshaven, not ironing beds squarely or leaving small droplets on the taps in the bathroom. They demanded such high levels of perfection that it was easy to fail.

With such high levels demanded of us it was easy to find flaws, particularly considering that there were over 80 young guys in the unit who had come from all parts of the country, fresh out of school and had grown up in different types of homes.

The level of self-discipline between individuals was quite variable. Some people were extremely slack and regularly let the team down, while others were highly disciplined and ended up picking up what the slackers left in their wake.

But you can't always carry others, somewhere somehow there are going to be gaps created; flaws in performance that will get noticed. These were the infringements picked up by the corporals and officers, which meant we were daily subjected to physical punishment.

To some people this punishment was unbearable. I heard that in the worst cases there were people who committed suicide. These were the individuals who had underlying undetected psychopathology who when subjected to daily intimidation and punishment eventually completely cracked under the pressure.

For the rest of us, we all suffered through and kept going. Fortunately for me, there were many other individuals who had much less mental toughness, or possibly fewer coping mechanisms, and would crack under pressure well before I ever did. This meant that I was let off the hook because a sign that other people were beginning to crack meant that the punishment session was going to end soon.

What I noticed during those times was that we all have certain thresholds for discomfort, pain and difficulty. Once that threshold is reached we tend to give up and fold. During those times of punishment, I would just bide my time and wait for the low threshold people to start breaking, complaining and giving up.

This is one example how mental toughness can help you get an easier ride through life. People with mental toughness can persevere longer through tough and difficult situations. When others give up, mentally tough people push on. Usually, this alone is the reason for their success. So many times the difference between the person who wins and the one who fails is as narrow as the razors edge. Below you will find several ideas you can use to develop more mental toughness, to ensure you push to the end when others give up.

Meditation

Your mind is the ultimate battle ground. It is here that you make or break. A disciplined mind, can lead to a disciplined life.

Your mind is always active; thoughts are constantly circulating through your brain, up to 70,000 per day. Sometimes it gets awfully noisy up there amongst all the clamour and racket.

We need to develop strategies to quieten down all that internal noise, so that we can regain focus on what's most important. One such strategy is through meditation.

Meditation can be as simple as concentrating on your breathing for 60 seconds or counting the 'seconds' hand on a clock for a minute. During this time you concentrate on nothing less. If you find your mind wandering, simply bring it back to your focal point.

This will discipline your mind by focussing your thoughts onto a particular point. Our minds are generally undisciplined, so people who are capable of maintaining greater control over their thoughts and concentration, will be more capable of achieving greater things.

Most people never take the time to discipline their minds, which is why so few achieve more than mediocre results at best.

There are many benefits to meditation.[72] Studies suggest that meditation increases activation in the ventromedial prefrontal cortex, the area of the brain that controls worrying.[88] It also increases activity in the anterior cingulate cortex which governs thinking and emotion. The effect of this extra activation is to reduce anxiety and worry.

Many religions of the world have been employing the benefits of meditation for centuries. Scientists have been slowly catching up to what these practitioners have known all along.

Meditation introduces more discipline into your life because it forces you to silence your mind, focus your attention and control the distractions in your noisy head.

Physical Activity

Another area which is supported by science to toughen you up is exercise. Activities like weight lifting, running and swimming are effective in strengthening your self-discipline.

To achieve greater benefits from exercise you should push your limits. Weight lifters do this all the time. They have a buddy 'spot' them while they do very heavy lifts, to the point of muscle failure. At this point the 'spotter' helps them complete the lift. Once their muscles recover after some rest, they come back stronger and bigger. They come back with the ability to push heavier weights than before.

One important caution is to maintain your form. Bad form can cause injury, which will put an end to your exercise for some time. You should always think sustainability when embarking on an exercise routine. Plan to be doing exercise years from now, and therefore create a sustainable program now which you can be doing long into the future.

You can utilise the benefits of meditation and exercise together to achieve greater limits. For example in the army they would make us do diamond press-ups until our arms ached and shivered from exhaustion. We had to hold the push-up position until our arms started to collapse.

What I used to do was concentrate on my breathing, or place my mind elsewhere other than my arms. It would take my mind off the discomfort in my body and redirect it to a more harmonious and tranquil place. In this state, I could hold the push-up position well past the point of most of my comrade's breaking point.

Cold Exposure

Studies show that exposure to cold leads to rapid and intense rise in adrenaline.[21]

Taking cold showers or ice baths will help you to strengthen your resolve and toughen you up to deal with stressful situations.

If you don't like the idea of being exposed solely to cold water, you can try alternating it with warm water; 30 seconds cold then 30 seconds warm, over and over.

Fasting

Another means of toughening up your mind and body is through fasting. This not only improves your health, but also makes you tougher mentally. The benefits of fasting are supported by science.[40]

There are various ways of fasting. You can fast 24, 48 or 72 hours flat. You can fast 1 meal for a week. It is all up to you. However, before you do any fasting, particularly if you are concerned, first discuss how suitable fasting is for you with your medical professional.

When you fast you take charge of your body rather than your body taking charge of you. Rather than reacting to our stomachs, we force it to be subject to our will. Remember that the spirit is willing but the body is weak. Don't be controlled by your appetite.

Force yourself to do uncomfortable things

We are so averse to feeling uncomfortable that we miss literally countless opportunities in life. Jeff Olson, author of *The Slight Edge: Secret to a Successful Life* says that, "Successful people do what unsuccessful people are not willing to do."

Consider what things you are not willing to do but which would triple your chances of achieving your most important goals. Things like:

- Talking to complete strangers
- Singing in public
- Giving a speech
- Doing an extreme sport
- Facing your fear of heights

These discomforts may create barriers which block your goals. It is not the case that successful people don't feel uncomfortable about doing uncomfortable things, like everyone else they do, but they have developed the mental toughness to tolerate these situations.

Don't Wait Until You 'Feel Like It'

If you wait until you feel like it, then you might be waiting a very long time before you get started on your dreams.

Often I don't feel like going out for a run, particularly on a cold frosty winters day, but I go anyway. It's cold to get started, but soon my body warms up and I feel great. If I waited for my body to feel like running, I never would.

If we rely on our feelings to motivate us, we will be waiting a long time indeed. Motivation comes from action. Get up and get moving first and then you will notice your motivation kicking in.

Author and motivational speaker, Zig Ziglar says, "You don't have to be great to start, but you have to start to be great".

No one (as far as I know) has ever suggested that you sit around and wait until you feel like getting off the couch before taking action on your most important dreams and desires.

The truth is, your feelings and motivation will match your behaviour as soon as you get busy working on your goals.

Complete Your Journal Daily

Make it your goal every day to complete your journal.

Every day for at least 90 days, take the time to fill out your journal. You might have to get up earlier, at least 30 minutes, if your day is already too busy. This is probably the most important first step in getting closer to achieving your dreams.

If you can't or won't commit to this first step, you will be sending all the wrong messages to your subconscious mind. It is like saying to yourself that your goals are not important because you are unwilling to do the things necessary to achieve them. This is not a good first start on your road to a better life. Rather send the right messages to your subconscious mind.

Every day write out your most important goals. Doing this will continually imprint the importance of these goals into your subconscious mind. You will start taking your goals more seriously than you have ever done before.

Each day define the next step towards achieving your goals, particularly your No 1 Goal. In David Allen's book, *Getting Things Done,*[4] he believes that the greatest secret to effective time management, is defining the next step. Determining what the next action is to take. Hence, your task is to define what your next action step is in the pursuit of your goals.

You should regularly remind yourself of your personal mission statement. Imprint it on your mind, and be able to recall it at the drop of a hat.

You should regularly take stock of your progress. Write out your recent advancements and achievements. This will serve as valuable evidence that you are making progress, taking new ground and advancing into areas you have never achieved before.

KEY POINTS TO REMEMBER

- Self-discipline does not come naturally to most of us. We have to learn and develop it as we grow up. The environment in which you grow up makes a big impact on how you view self-discipline and it may also determine how self-disciplined you are later in life.

- Self-discipline often gets a negative rap, because many people believe developing more self-discipline will be associated with pain and discomfort. The truth is that the discomfort you may have to endure to develop more self-discipline will pale in comparison to the benefits you will gain from having more self-discipline.

- The size of your goals will be in direct proportion to the amount of self-discipline you will need to achieve them. Big goals require big self-discipline. Being the champion of the world will require much greater self-discipline compared to being the champion in your local club.

- Greatness cannot be achieved without self-discipline. It is as important to success as air is to breathing. All great accomplishments and achievements emanated from the backs of people of self-discipline.

- Your habits and routines have the potential to elevate you to the top of your field. To develop and maintain these habits and routines will require self-discipline.

- There are many ways you can use to develop more self-discipline. One way is to put more controls around what you say. For instance you can filter everything you say by passing it through the GUT test of goodness, usefulness and truth.

- You can strengthen your mental toughness through various exercises like meditation, cold exposure, fasting, doing physical exercise and forcing yourself to do uncomfortable things. In this way you will discipline yourself to endure hardship longer and push yourself further.

- The general consensus is that motivation follows action, so get going first and your motivation will follow. Don't sit around waiting to feel like working on your goals. Doing this might leave you waiting for a very long time; so long that you may never start at all.

CHAPTER 10

Courage: Rise above your fears

"Your time is limited, so don't waste it living someone else's life. Don't be trapped by dogma - which is living with the results of other people's thinking. Don't let the noise of others' opinions drown out your own inner voice. And most important, have the courage to follow your heart and intuition."

Steve Jobs

How do you define courage? I define courage as the willingness to acknowledge your fears, and to rise to the challenge in spite of them.

Courage is also defined as bravery, boldness, having backbone, mettle and determination. The opposite of courage is cowardice and fear. Courage is essential to achieving your best self.

Courage is not the absence of fear. Everyone experiences fear, but courageous people are not incapacitated by it. They rise above their fears, and stand boldly in the face of them. Nobody can achieve their goals unless they can face their fears and overcome them, rather than have fear dominate their lives.

Chapter 10

Other People Can Sow Doubt And Fear Into Your Life

I once read a story about a man who lived on the side of the road and sold hot dogs. He did not have particularly good hearing so he didn't have a radio. As he also had trouble with his eyes, he didn't read the newspapers. But he was really good at selling hot dogs. He had an A-Frame sign on the side of the road advertising his hot dogs. He called out to people to come over and buy a hot dog. Everyone who tasted his hot dogs loved them and told their friends who likewise came over and bought his hot dogs.

Business was booming, so he put in more orders for meat and buns. He bought a bigger stove to take care of the extra demand. Eventually his son came back from college and began helping his dad in the business. But then something happened. His son said to him, "hey dad don't you know what's going on in the world today? It's all over the news. There is a huge recession going on. It's pretty bad. It's happening all over the world. Everyone is affected. It's terrible and our domestic situation is getting worse every day."

The boy's father thought to himself, "My son is well educated; he has been to college, so he must know what he is talking about." So the man cut back his orders, took down his A-Frame and stopped calling out to customers to buy his hot dogs. Soon business began to decline, his sales literally fell flat overnight.

"You're right son," said the man to his boy, "there really is a great depression going on."

The world is full of fearful people. They are infectious and can steal your joy, positivity and happiness. They can rob you of your goals and set you on a path to failure. To counteract their negative effects will require courage.

Courageous people have the ability to stand up and say "no!" People won't like that, and they won't like you for doing it. They

213

want you to conform. In fact, they need you to conform. If you don't it makes them feel uncomfortable. It fires up their fears. They want you to conform because it is in their best interests, and not yours. It makes their world more predictable and stable.

But conforming will most likely take you in the opposite direction to where you want to go. To achieve your own goals and forge your own path will require you to take risks. Unless you do, you will accomplish nothing in life – so said the late Muhammad Ali. Actor Christopher Reeve once said, "Either you decide to stay in the shallow end of the pool or you go out in the ocean."

So where will you swim? Will you stay in the paddling pool or swim out into the deep. Master Painter Vincent Van Gogh once said, "What would life be if we had no courage to attempt anything?" Well life would be pretty dark because we wouldn't have electricity or the light bulb. It would be slow because we wouldn't have motor vehicles or aeroplanes. We would be uneducated and ignorant because we wouldn't have books, pens or the internet to share information on. All these inventions required courage on behalf of the ones inventing them. All of them required going against convention and the ability to think differently. The people who invented the light bulbs, aeroplanes and automobiles had many challenges to overcome, critics to contend with, fears to conquer, that without courage they would have certainly failed.

In this chapter we will explore courage through two wonderful stories which highlight several important aspects. In the next story we will look at the lives of a group of painters who had to show courage and go against convention and resist conforming to achieve their dreams.

The Plight Of The Impressionists

The story about the beginning of impressionism is a good example of what it takes to step out on your own and forge a new path to achieve your goals. T. S. Eliot remarked, "If you do not take risks, you will never discover the full reaches of your potential. Only those who will risk going too far can possibly find out how far one can go." You can either spend your entire life living in the shadow of others, or step into the light yourself and create your own shadow.

Around 150 years ago, Paris was universally recognised as the art capital of the world. There were a splendid assortment of boulevards, cafes, restaurants and concert halls all over the city, catering for all sorts of customers. Back then a group of painters would gather every evening at café Guerbois to lament the frustrating situation they found themselves in. In those days, art was a closely regulated profession with many controls on what artists were allowed to do. It was fairly difficult for artists to exercise their creative liberties, without some form of restriction.

The group's leader was Edouard Manet who in his early thirties was the oldest of the group. Manet was a gregarious man, well dressed, handsome and fashionable. He was full of energy, charming and had a good sense of humour. His best friend was Edgar Degas, who was intelligent and could match Manet in wit and argument. Other members were Paul Cézanne, who would sit moodily in the corner, and Claude Monet, a grocer's son, who was strong willed, and self-absorbed. Monet was not as well educated as some Pierre-Auguste Renoir of the other members of the group and his best friend would paint portraits of him. Camille Pissarro was the group's moral compass. He was interested in politics, was a loyal friend and had strong principles. He was well loved by the other members of the group. The group was close knit. They painted one another, painted next to each other and supported each other emotionally and financially.

This group of painters were ordinary, law abiding citizens. They were no different from you and I. They had dreams and desires and wanted to make something of their lives. For them a good start would have been to communicate their artistic expressions in a way they wanted to.

Today their works hang in every major museum in the world and are worth Billions. But back in the 1860's they were poor, struggling and unknown. No dealers were interested in their paintings and the small army of art critics who existed in Paris would normally belittle and demean their work. They had an almost impossible summit to climb in getting the powers that be to recognise their artistic style as legitimate.

What is obvious about their situation is that it resembles many of our own. We all have obstacles and challenges ahead of us, if we decide to pursue our passions and dreams it will be fraught with difficulty and upward battle.

Back in the 19th century art played a big role in the cultural lives of the people living in Paris. The government had a regulatory body in place, The Imperial House and the Fine Arts, who regulated the art profession. It was much like the regulatory bodies of today, who regulate professions like medicine and law. Artists had to go through rigorous training and spend years climbing the ranks. Students started with copying drawings and progressed to painting live models. There were competitions at every stage of an artist's development which was used to weed out the good artists from the bad. One of the most important goals artists had was to one day exhibit their work in the Salon. The Salon was the most important exhibition in all of Europe.

Each year painters would submit 1 or 2 of their best works to a jury of experts by the 1st of April. At that time there were roughly

3000 painters in France, so there was a small mountain of paintings to grade at each exhibition. Over several weeks the panel would consider each work and vote. Unacceptable work got rejected, while the lucky few got hung in the exhibition on the walls of the Palais for 6 weeks starting in May. The Palais was an enormous structure, 274 meters long and 2 stories high. Typically the Salon would accept 3000 – 4000 paintings hung in 4 tiers. Paintings which had received unanimous agreement from the jury were hung at eye level. If artists' works were "skyed" placed on the top level, it was almost as if their work wasn't exhibited at all, because at that level works were practically out of sight.

Thousands of people would visit the exhibition over the proceeding weeks. They would fuss and revere some works and ridicule and disrespect others. Works which received high praise saw sale prices soar and the artist got a huge boost in fame. The Salon had a huge grip on an artist's future. It could make or break an artist's reputation.

The situation for the impressionists was bleak. Renoir wrote to his friend Durard-Ruel, "there were scarcely fifteen art lovers capable of liking a painting without the backing of the Salon and there are another 80,000 who won't buy so much as a postcard unless the painter exhibits there. That's why every year I send two portraits, however small. The entry is entirely of a commercial nature. Anyway, it's like some medicine– if it does you no good, it will do you no harm." Hence, without the Salons approval, artists had very little chance of selling anything at all.

The Salon exerted huge power over an artist's future and most painters applied themselves diligently to satisfying the demands of the Salons conventions. To not do so would almost certainly have meant committing career suicide. The Salon was the supreme selling place, where reputations were made and prices were set for artists work. The fear of stepping out on their own trapped artists into maintaining the conventions and whims of others.

The Salon exerted power over artist's creative ambitions. Sue Roe[35] an art historian states that, "Works were expected to be microscopically accurate, properly finished and formally framed, with proper perspective and all the familiar artistic conventions." From the Salons perspective, the public needed to be entertained. Artworks needed to meet viewer's expectations. Usually acceptable art pieces were large depictions of historical scenes, or mythical in nature, with horses, armies and beautiful woman. But this was not what the impressionists had in mind to paint. They preferred to paint everyday scenes, with broad brushstrokes. To people who visited the Salon their work looked amateurish and even shocking. For example, in 1865, to his great surprise, Manet got one of his paintings accepted to the Salon. It was a painting of a prostitute called Olympia. The work shocked the art world in Paris to its core. The Salon had to place guards to keep the crowds at bay. Historian Ross King claims the painting caused mass hysteria with some spectators collapsing in fits of uncontrollable laughter. Still others turned their heads in fright.

The Salon was the biggest game in town and unless artists conformed their art works to the will of the Salon, they would be left on the outside, to struggle in obscurity and insignificance. To cede to the demands of the Salon would certainly mean to get lost in the clutter of all the other works. There was no individualism, no distinction, it all looked the same. This was the world the impressionists found themselves in. They had spent many years battling against the machine. They were getting nowhere. They needed to do something different.

The Rise Above The Machine

Great reward requires great courage. Fear can keep you trapped and unless you take the plunge you will never achieve your biggest dreams and highest goals. The impressionists knew this and so eventually, the group started to debate going it alone. They discussed setting up their own show and running their own exhibition. They would be attempting something never attempted before. After all, who would dare to go up against the mighty Salon! It was a risk; it was fraught with danger and uncertainty. Doubtless the impressionists were plagued with fear and trepidation. Manet was against the whole idea; he believed in the Salons purpose. Pissaro and Monet disagreed. They believed it was better to step out and start their own show. They were tired of being lost in the crowd and the restrictions imposed on them by the Salon. They wanted something new.

Someone once said, "Never be afraid to try something new. Remember, amateurs built the ark, professionals built the Titanic." Maybe your fear is based on the notion that because no one else considers your idea worthy, that somehow it isn't. Henry Ford once remarked, "One of the greatest discoveries a man makes, one of his great surprises, is to find he can do what he was afraid he couldn't do."

Finally, in 1873, Pissaro and Monet took decisive action. They proposed the group set up their own collective called the Société anonyme des artistes, peintres, sculpteurs, graveurs, etc. There would be no competitions, juries or medals. Artists could hang whatever they liked. All artists were equal. Everyone, bar Manet was in.

The group found a vacant space in a building recently vacated by photographer Nadar on the second floor of 35 Boulevard des Capucines. On the 15th of April, 1874 they launched their first exhibition which lasted 1 month. The exhibition featured more than 200 works. Among the exhibitionists were Cézanne, who displayed 3 works, Degas 10 works, Monet 5 canvases and 7 sketches, Pissaro 5 works, Renoir 6 works and Alfred Sisley 5 works. Three thousand people attended the show, 175 in the first day alone. The show was big enough to attract the attention of the artist critics. Some reviews were positive, others not so much.

One critic said it looked as if the artists took a pistol, loaded it with paint and fired it at a canvas.

In the history of modern art, this was the most important and famous exhibition of all time. If you tried to purchase those paintings today, you would be in for a hefty bill of well over $1 billion dollars.

Once upon a time, people laughed at the idea that humans would fly. Now we have landed on the moon. We have sent probes to the furthest reaches of our solar system. One day in the not too distant future we will establish a colony on Mars. It takes courage to go after your goals in the face of criticism and disapproval. We like to conform because it is the easiest road to follow. It's the safe route. But it ends in living a life of unfulfilled dreams and unrealised desires.

In the next story we will consider the account of a young boy who decided to take the hard road fraught with peril and risk, but who had the courage to attempt the impossible and won.

The Boy Who Would Slay The Giant

The story of David and Goliath is a well-known account of courage and bravery. Irrespective of your religion or particular faith, there is much to be learned about courage from this story. The story of David and Goliath goes back to antiquity, yet continues to inspire people around the world today. The story was so inspiring that the great artist Michelangelo created a statue of David in Italy and the famous painter Caravaggio created a painting of David holding Goliath's head. The story has been etched into history and the minds of millions of people worldwide.

The story of David and Goliath starts in ancient Palestine in the Valley of Elah (see 1 Samuel 17). It was here that the armies of Israel faced off with their long-time enemies, the Philistines. The Israelites were encamped along the northern ridge of the Elah, while the Philistines occupied the southern ridge. Both armies were stalled; no one wanted to go down into the more vulnerable valley, as that would give their enemy an advantage from above. After sometime, the Philistines made a move by sending their best warrior forward to lay down a challenge. To settle the stalemate, he invited Israel to send down their best warrior to battle it out, man to man.

But no one from the Israelite army was willing to take up the challenge. Just one look at Goliath and you would have known why. Goliath was an infantry man, a unit which specialised in hand to hand combat. They were big men, with heavy armour and specialised weapons with which to cut down their opponents. Goliath was their top fighter. He was a giant of a man, around 9 foot tall (3 meters), and he wore body armour which weighed 57kg. No one from the Israelite army was willing to go down and face him, as it would have meant certain death. Well no one except one person; a small shepherd boy named David stepped forth to volunteer.

At that time David was acting as a type of errand boy, going back and forth to his home to collect and then deliver food to his 3 older brothers who had enlisted in the Israelite army. David was not a soldier; rather he was a young shepherd boy who had no military training. Reluctantly the leader of the Israelite army, King Saul agreed – after some convincing though – as David explained that he had taken out Lions and Bears before, when they attacked the flock of sheep he tended. To David, Goliath was just another beast which could be slain. What's more, Goliath had challenged God, and this was something David could not accept. His challenge needed to be answered, David's motivation for fighting Goliath had moved to a much higher purpose. He wanted to show God's glory in battle.

So David headed into battle, with only his sling shot, a few smooth stones and a stick. When Goliath saw the stick that David was carrying he shouted, "Am I a dog that you come to me with sticks?" (1 Samuel 17:43; NIV), and Goliath confidently believed that David's weapons were puny and useless against his might.

When Goliath saw him approaching, he yelled out at David "Come here," he said, "and I'll give your flesh to the birds and the wild animals!"(1 Samuel 17:44; NIV). Goliath was super confident that he was going to dispatch David with ease, like snapping a dry twig in his powerful hands.

We often need courage to face big bullies. We are bullied in many ways, by our peers in school, our siblings, our bosses, our spouses, our neighbours. We get bullied by the government, big organisations, and corporations. It can come from all angles, which can stifle our courage and instil fear deep within us. Most of the time, bullies appear like giants, who seem too big to conquer.

But David did not intend to go and meet Goliath on his field of battle. He did not intend to fight Goliath on his terms - and for good reason. David was an expert with the slingshot, not with the sword. This was his greatest military strength. David was similar to a modern day sniper, able to pick off his enemy from a distance. He was as deadly with a slingshot, as Goliath was with a sword.

When I was writing this section I came to the realisation that David was the only answer Israel had for the Goliath problem. It was unlikely that there was anyone in Israel big and strong enough to face Goliath man to man. He was just too big and powerful. No ordinary human would be able to match him in close quarter combat. The only way to deal with such an enemy was to take him out from a distance, and who better to do that than an expert marksman with a slingshot. While in the wilderness, David would have protected his sheep from Lions and Bears. David developed expert level skill with the sling shot. I imagine he must have spent hours practicing hitting targets, and hunting prey while out alone in the fields. When you come down to it, David was Goliaths worst nightmare. He was precisely what Goliath did not expect.

David loaded a stone into his sling, and proceeded to swing it at full speed. He launched the projectile at Goliaths head. Goliath was as slow as he was big, so the stone found its target, smacking him straight in the forehead, breaking skull and bone with a mighty crack. The giant fell in a heap; his huge body littering the landscape. David ran up to him, picked up his mammoth sword and removed his head from his body. The world stood silent. The armies stood aghast. You could literally hear a pin drop. Then suddenly a huge roar of praise erupted from the Israelite ranks. They rushed down the embankment and attacked the dumbfounded Philistines with great force and confidence. The Philistines fell at their feet, and those who were not cut down fled. The battle was won. The victory was theirs. But none of that would have been possible had it not been for the young shepherd boy who had the courage to take on the Giant.

So what or who represents your greatest giants?

What are you afraid they will do to you?

Some people may think the story is a fable. A story told to children and adults to give them courage in tough times. There is plenty of evidence to show that the story was real; that the events that transpired that day told a tale of true courage.

There are many facts in the story which demonstrate its authenticity. Back in David's day, the slingshot was a fearsome weapon, feared in the ancient world. It has been estimated that a shot from a slingshot had the stopping power of a 45-caliber handgun[22, 43]. There was enough power to kill a person on impact. In ancient armies slingers, like archers formed part of the artillery divisions.

Medical experts speculate that Goliath may have had a medical condition known as "acromegaly"[6]. The condition is caused by a benign tumour of the pituitary gland. The condition would have caused the pituitary gland to overproduce the human growth hormone which would have contributed to Goliaths huge size. A further side effect of the condition was to cause problems with vision. This may have caused blurry vision. It has been speculated that the shield bearer was there to lead Goliath, as he couldn't see well. This would have effectively rendered Goliath a blind lumbering buffoon, being led to his death by his assistant.

Personally I don't buy this idea for one moment. Firstly, why would the Philistines put their faith in someone like that? He was holding their fate in the balance. Logics would suggest that they sent out their best warrior, the one with the best chance of gaining the upper hand and producing a victory. Secondly, Goliath does not appear to have any visual impediments, as he quite clearly sees David coming down to meet him in battle, with a stick in hand. We know David was quite some distance from him as his attack did not require close quarter combat. Goliath is clearly over-confident, bombastic and arrogant in the words he yells at David – which to me doesn't ring of a person who is lumbering and blind. And finally, if Goliath was so bent out of shape, why did no one else from the Israelite ranks volunteer to take him out. There was a sizeable reward offered for the man who would defeat the Giant.

Acting out in courage can end with great reward. The risk might be big but the reward even bigger.

Back in the day when the young David led his flock of sheep across the Israelite landscape, his occupation was considered to be one of the lowest of all. Shepherds were not held in high regard back then and even David was considered insignificant by his family (see the story of when the prophet Samuel visits his home in 1 Samuel 16). David was certainly not held in high esteem, and no one expected anything great would come from him. David had an opportunity. Defeating the giant would raise his profile and position in life. When you look back on the lives of many successful people, you discover that they rose up precisely because they were laid low. They were suppressed or disregarded and had nothing to lose. Their courage to rise up came as a result of their lack of comfort. How often do we get to a point where we have sufficient comforts around us to make us complacent? We have just enough to stop us trying harder or doing something new and different. David was not in that situation.

On the other hand, Goliath was a man held in high esteem. We know this because he was the man the Philistines chose to represent them in a battle; a battle which could decide their ultimate fate. Goliath was a man of great repute. He was famous, and most likely a superstar celebrity among his people. His fame extended across borders; the Bible gives us a great amount of detail about his armour, its size and weight. We know how tall Goliath was, and I imagine there were many other details known about him not recorded in scripture. Goliath was also a soldier, which means he was trained in the art of killing. He was an expert in close combat and was incredibly deadly.

When you consider all of the benefits Goliath had, it is apparent that he required much less courage than David. This indifference may have been a decisive factor in his demise.

When we do something new for the first time it requires more courage than when we have done it several times before. We grow in self-confidence and this reduces our fears. Virgil Thomson says, "Try a thing you haven't done three times. Once, to get over the fear of doing it. Twice, to learn how to do it. And a third time to figure out whether you like it or not."

The only real way to develop more courage is to face your fear. Here is a small, young man attempting to do battle with a Giant. Everyone else had run for cover. No one was willing to risk their lives against such a foe. Author Dale Carnegie says, "Inaction breeds doubt and fear. Action breeds confidence and courage. If you want to conquer fear, do not sit at home and think about it. Go out and get busy." David knew this, and he loaded his sling.

So what challenge do you need to vanquish in your life? Will you be like David and face it head on or like the rest of Saul's army and hide? Will you place your comfort, ego or pride ahead of your dreams and desires, or will the cost exacted by them rob you of living the life you deserve.

Following David's miraculous triumph over Goliath, he eventually became King of Israel. He is remembered in history precisely because of his courageous actions. This is true of many of the other individuals from the past who have attempted courageous acts. People like Hillary and Norgay, Scott and Amundsen, Nelson Mandella, Winston Churchill, and Jesus, to name a few. People who walked the path others were to too afraid to walk. People who laid their lives on the line and risked it all to reach their highest goals and greatest objectives.

Very few people from that day are recorded in scripture. Most were afraid and hid from the challenge. Some were critical and biting. No one builds a statue to a critic. None of their names were recorded. Their cowardice resulted in living lives of mediocrity, which no one cares about. Courage takes you out of mediocrity. You get noticed. You make a difference and play a key role in the welfare of others. Look back on history, people with courage made a difference, they got remembered, they got respected.

The Conquest Of Fear

Gandhi once said, "The enemy is fear. We think it is hate; but, it is fear." I believe Gandhi was correct; fear is the greatest enemy to your success. If fear is the only thing getting between you and your highest goal, then there is nothing between you and your highest goal.

Let me explain. Fear is an emotion, it is not a tangible object. Psychologists claim we have primarily six emotions: Joy, Surprise, Sadness, Anger, Disgust, and Fear.[84] These 6 are universally recognised. Each of these emotions have practical use for the survival of the human race. Fear acts like a type of alarm bell, sounding off when you get into a threatening or dangerous situation. When you experience fear, you have a physiological response with certain chemicals flooding into your brain. You get ready to react. You take measures to protect yourself.

For instance, you have started a new exercise program of walking three times per week. On one such occasion you are walking along the sidewalk in your neighbourhood on a peaceful afternoon. The sun is high in the sky and the day is calm and warm. Suddenly you hear a rushing sound charging up to the fence beside you. You turn to see a big, ugly aggressive canine jump up onto the fence, growling and barking. It would like nothing more than to take a chunk out of you. You brace yourself, pull back away from the fence. Your body floods with adrenaline. You get ready to run. But, it's okay. Fortunately the dog can't break through the fence. You are safe. Your peaceful afternoon doesn't seem so peaceful anymore. You feel shaken. You just experienced a flight response which was triggered by the fear emotion. Fear is useful in these situations. Its helps us escape danger.

Now you don't want to go for a walk anymore. Every time you think about going out you relive the same situation. You see those big teeth lashing out at you. You feel the tension in your body. You feel a rush of adrenaline. No dog is present for you to experience the same physiological reaction as you did before. Your thoughts are enough. So you stop walking and throw your exercise program out. Fear has got you trapped. It has incapacitated you. Notice it is not the dog which has incapacitated you, it is your irrational fear, and the mountain of excuses you now sell yourself to justify it.

In Robert Leahy's book, "The worry cure: Seven steps to stop worry from stopping you"[54] he refers to a study in which subjects were asked to write down their worries over a period of time and then identify the incidents which happened. Interestingly 85% of subjects worries did not happen, and from the 15% whose worry did eventuate, 79% discovered they could handle the situation better than they thought they would, or they found that the expected difficulty taught them a valuable lesson. Essentially their worry was in their minds alone. They were not real. For millions of people, worry and fear will continue to stifle their achievements and rob them of their goals. So what do you do to change this situation?

Here is a process you can follow to better manage fear and reduce its impact on you achieving your best self. Firstly, identify your fear, then acknowledge it and finally face it.

1. Identify the fear

In the previous example, the trigger was the aggressive dog. It was easy to identify the source in this case because it was blatantly obvious. But on many occasions it is much more difficult to identify the source of our fears. The source may not be so obvious. The source may be your own irrational thinking which you use to maintain it. Likewise, the source may be irrational beliefs. For instance, a fear of going to the mailbox due to the possibility of been hit by a meteor. Some people experience this very fear, and most of us have our own irrational versions. The secret to overcoming fear is to identify it. Call it by name and you will have taken most of the power it has over you. David's source of fear was Goliath; the Impressionist source was The Salon. But identifying your fear is not enough. It is insufficient to simply know what you scared of as this does not change your predicament in a meaningful manner.

2. Acknowledge your fear

Once you have identified the source of your fear, acknowledge it. Take ownership of it. Don't try to deny it. You will use far more cognitive energy trying to suppress it with rationalisations and excuses. It will be more exhausting keeping it suppressed than letting it out. I know it can be embarrassing admitting that we are not as tough as we would like others and ourselves to believe. But I think it takes a much tougher person to admit your weaknesses. The interesting thing is that people will come to respect you more, and you will be seen as a more credible and authentic when you can admit your weaknesses and fears. But most importantly, you will be in a better position to deal with your fear.

3. Face your fear

Now that you have identified your fear and acknowledged it to yourself and others, you can face it. It's your fear after all, so own it. Facing you fear means you are not mastered by it. On the contrary, it means you take control of it. You can work on ways to deal with it, and possibly even eradicate it all together from your life. You will have to risk some of your comforts. Frederick Wilcox says, "Progress always involves risks. You can't steal second base and keep your foot on first."

Both the impressionists and David faced what appeared, impossible odds. The giants would have only remained impossible had they not found the courage to face them. They took great risk and attempted great feats of bravery. Their stories are accounts of courage. For the other participants in these stories, theirs were not tales of courage, but rather of cowardice. Their fear kept them trapped. They were immobilised by it and condemned to live lives of conformance and mediocrity. Few are remembered today. To achieve your best self will require courage. It will necessitate meeting new challenges head on, rising above your fears and taking greater risks.

KEY POINTS TO REMEMBER

- Courage is the willingness to acknowledge your fears, and rise to your challenges in spite of them. The opposite of courage is fear. Nobody can achieve their highest goals unless they can face their fear and prevent it from dominating their lives.

- Our fears may appear like powerful giants which are impossible to slay. All giants have a weakness and can be brought down and defeated. Your job is find that weakness and exploit it.

- It takes courage to go after your goals in the face of criticism and disapproval. We like to conform because it is the easiest road to follow. It's the safe route. It ends in living a life of unfulfilled dreams and unrealised desires.

- To achieve your best self will require courage. It will necessitate meeting new challenges head on, rising above your fear and taking greater risks.

- Many people seem to build their lives on a foundation of fear.

CHAPTER 11

Procrastinating: Get started on your goals now!

"Do you know what happens when you give a procrastinator a good idea? Nothing!"

Donald Gardner

Procrastination is the tendency to put off till tomorrow, that which should be done today.

When you procrastinate, you routinely do tasks either at the very last minute, after the due deadline, or not at all. Statistics suggest 95% of people admit to procrastinating, so you are in good company if you are one of the many who leave things to the last minute, or don't do them at all.

Windy Dryden, author of *Overcoming Procrastination*,[24] gives a really good definition of what procrastination is; "people procrastinate when they routinely give more weight to the short term advantages of avoiding doing what is in their best interests to do, than to the long term advantages of doing the task concerned." Another way of looking at is to say that procrastination has short term rewards but costs you in the long run.

Procrastination is not a mental disorder nor a disease, but chronic procrastination can be a consequence of a diagnosable mental disorder, like depression or anxiety. For most people, procrastination is simply the tendency to avoid doing tasks and jobs which are not particularly enjoyable; or tasks that seem overly large or difficult. We all have tasks we would rather not do, like cleaning the toilet, writing an essay, studying for a test, throwing out the rubbish, phoning an irate customer, changing the oil in the car or doing the dishes.

I've been in some houses where I can assure you that the residents were big procrastinators when it came to washing the dishes and cleaning the kitchen. In one house I once visited, dishes were everywhere, all over the counter tops, on the table and strewn over the shelves. There were no dishes left in the cupboards. The house was a big boarding house with 8 rooms and no single person was willing to take responsibility for the kitchen, so everyone simply dissolved themselves of all responsibility and the place just went into total disarray and chaos.

The point is that procrastination has consequences, and in most cases the costs are negative. Many people who keep putting off doing the important things in life, achieve far less than their lives deserve. Here are some typical day to day consequences of delaying doing what you should be doing now:

Nine Ways Procrastination Can Cost You Time, Money And Health

1. Costs you your health

Numerous studies have documented the effects of procrastination on health. For example two longitudinal studies examined the effects of procrastination on student's health.[77] At the beginning of the semester, procrastinators reported lower levels of stress and illness than non-procrastinators, but this trend quickly changed as the semester drew on. By the end of the semester procrastinators reported higher levels of stress and illness than non-procrastinators and were overall sicker. The researchers concluded that procrastination is a self-defeating behaviour which is characterised by short term gain and long term costs.[77] Not writing your essay when there is plenty of time in the tank might feel good right now, but the picture soon turns bleaker when the tank is empty and the deadline is looming. Psychologist William James once said, "Nothing is as fatiguing as the eternal hanging on of an uncompleted task."

2. Costs more on credit card fees

Here is a good example of how procrastination will literally cost you money. What happens when you pay your credit card late? The Bank slaps you with a late payment fee of $25 for example. If you pay your credit card late 3 times a year that is an extra $75 you have wasted through procrastination. Not to mention the extra stress and annoyance of seeing the extra charges appearing on your bank statement – I know this because it has happened to me. This can all be avoided by paying your credit card on time. Christopher Parker says, "Procrastination is like a credit card: it's a lot of fun until you get the bill."

3. Costs valuable time

Procrastination waists time, and as time is your most precious resource, procrastination can be extremely costly. Benjamin Franklin said, "You may delay, but time will not, and lost time is never found again". Time is your most precious resource; it is more valuable than money, gold, silver or precious stones. Time is the most valuable gift you can ever give to another person; because once you have given it you can never get it back again. Charles Dickens advice is "to never do tomorrow what you can do today. Procrastination is the thief of time." Generally we protect ourselves from thieves; we lock our cars and homes, install alarm systems and remain vigilant in risky places. So why not protect yourself from procrastination the same way you protect your property and your life!

4. You buy gifts at the last minute

When you wait until the last minute to buy gifts you invariably rush around rather than take your time shopping. Instead of getting a good deal you end up spending far more than you intended to. Imagine the annoyance, crying and disappointment of your 6 year old who has been nagging you for months for that new gismo and when you finally go to the shop to get one, they are all sold out. Alternatively you have missed the special and now have to pay full price. Once again procrastination has cost you money. Max Brooks says, "If you believe you can accomplish everything by 'cramming' at the eleventh hour, by all means, don't lift a finger now. But you may think twice about beginning to build your ark once it has already started raining."

5. You pay more for Air Tickets

If you do a lot of flying you will know what I am taking about right here. Leaving the booking of your air ticket to the very last minute really adds up the cost. You might pay double or triple the price of a ticket purchased a few weeks in advance. On some airlines the ticket prices go up daily. It's all based on supply and demand, as soon as tickets get sold; the available seats are reduced and become more valuable. The price you see today will have gone up by tomorrow.

6. Delay your retirement savings

Here is one which will cost you severely. The sooner you start saving for your retirement the more money you will have waiting for you when you retire. Many people delay their savings until it's too late to make any measurable difference. Instead of several hundred thousand dollars waiting in their retirement account, they have barely enough for a year's income. Don't wait for tomorrow, start saving now.

7. You more on shipping costs

When you leave it too long to make that purchase of stationary, stock or products when you have almost run out, you end up having to pay extra for the overnight delivery charges. Do that enough times and you notice the negative effect on your bottom line. When you fail to order your supplies on time you end up having to ship via the overnight or express methods which cost significantly more. Instead of $3 dollars you end up paying $30. Procrastination results in money lost once again.

8. Filing your taxes late will incur late filing fees or fines

When you are late filing your taxes you get hit with interest charges, or late filing penalties. In 2002, it is reported that 40 % of Americans waited too long to file their taxes, missed the deadline and got a nice $400 fine. That's a huge loss of personal income due to procrastination. Imagine the millions of extra revenue the IRS pulled in that year without lifting a finger. The more you delay filing your taxes the happier the tax man becomes. Your procrastination is money in the bank for someone else.

9. Costs you your business or home

How many people keep putting off taking out insurance until it is too late? They keep putting off that house or car insurance until the fateful day when something nasty happens. Then there is the case when your insurance renewal is coming due and instead of phoning around to get updated quotes from other companies who could offer you better rates, you procrastinate to the point where you have to renew your current policy to maintain cover.

Thirteen Key Tips To Overcome Procrastination

1. Eat that Elephant

For some people the obstacles standing in their path are so large, they seem like very large elephants. Now imagine you had to eat an elephant to get it out of your path. Ordinarily, eating an elephant in one go would be a huge undertaking for any one person to embark on.

For a whole village not so much of a problem, but for a single individual it is a huge job. People tend to view a job like this as so large that they don't even start on it. It seems insurmountable, overwhelming or impossible, so they just leave it alone, and go find something else easier to do; like sitting in front of the telly with a bowl of potato chips.

Take for instance writing a book. According to an article published by journalist Joseph Epstein, in The New York Times, a recent survey revealed that 81% of Americans felt they had a book they wanted to write. Very few ever got started. Out of every 1,000 people who start writing a book, only 30 finish, and then to top it off, out of the 30 that complete their book, only 6 go on to publish it. I imagine that writing a book looks like a very big elephant to most people, and big elephants are really intimidating, particularly if you have to eat it all in one gulp.

But what if you could cut the elephant up into many, many small pieces? If you only ate one small piece at a time, the task would not only become psychologically smaller, but it would also become physically more achievable.

For instance, if you decided to write only 500 words per day, which is what you can typically fit on an A4 page with 10 – 12 font size, you would produce 182,500 words per annum, and considering a typical non-fiction book is anything from 50,000 to

70,000 words, you would have at least 3 books written by the end of the year. If you decide to only write ¾ of the days in a year, which is roughly 275 days, you would produce approximately 137,000 words, enough to fill 2 non- fiction books or 1 pretty large fiction book.

The key here is to take a very large task, project or goal and break it down into very small, manageable parts and then work on one part at a time until it is completed. The small wins you experience from completing all the individual parts will provide you with a huge psychological and emotional boost, which will push you on to completing more and more of the undertaking. Before you know it you will have eaten the entire elephant.

Resolve today to take a large goal and break it into several sub-goals, and then start working on each sub goal until complete.

---

2. Eat that frog

In Brian Tracy's book, *Eat That Frog,*[78] he proposes one way to deal with procrastination is to eat a frog at the very beginning of the day.

Who wants to eat a frog? Yuk, how awful! And that's the whole point of the exercise. By doing the worst of your tasks or jobs first thing in the morning the rest of your day is clear of un- pleasantries and you can get on with enjoying your day far sooner.

So the advice here is to do the jobs you tend to procrastinate on, first thing in the morning, and you will improve your productivity. Now just think about that for a minute. How would you improve your productivity if you did the worst job first?

When you have an unpleasant task, like eating a frog, you will most likely put that task at the very end of the day. Your natural tendency will be to leave it till the last moment. So everything else slows down as you push the point in time further away when you have to complete an un-enjoyable task.

If you eat the frog first, there will be nothing slowing you down and you can speed up your productivity as a result. What if you have to eat two or more frogs on the same day, Tracy offers a workable solution, eat the ugliest frog first.

Resolve today to cut procrastination at the roots by completing the most unpleasant tasks first thing, thereby freeing yourself to do the more enjoyable tasks later.

3. Face your fears

In their book *Procrastination: Why you do it, what to do about it now* authors Burka and Yuen believe a large part of why people procrastinate is due to fear.[12] People fear all sorts of things, including success and failure.

Since you were a child the world has pulled a veil of fear over your life. You picked up all sorts of negative messages and introjected them. Since before you can remember people have told you, "you can't do it", "it's too risky", "it won't work", and "it's too hard" which has had the effect of sabotaging your dreams. From what you have picked up from others you may have introjected messages like;

- success will demand too much of me
- I can't do what's required of me
- success is dangerous, someone will get hurt
- success is off limits
- I don't deserve it

The biggest obstacle in your life which might be standing in your way is fear. To some people fear is a complete waste of time. Loa Tzu once said, "There is no illusion greater than fear."

If fear is only an illusion then it does not exist, it is a figment of your imagination, and if it does not exist then why should you be afraid or worse allow it to hold so much power over you. This is most likely why Franklin D. Roosevelt said, "The only thing we have to fear is fear itself", because fear itself is the obstacle that many cannot ascend.

Fear for many is the barrier which is too hard to scale, the mountain too tough to summit. If you truly want to overcome your fear you need to act on it, rather than be paralyzed by it, as W. Clement Stone says, "Thinking will not overcome fear but action will."

Only through action will you climb the mountain, push through the ice and snow and reach the summit. Only through action will you reach the top, see the view and achieve your dreams. To do anything less is to fail, and if it is failure you fear, then take some advice from Actor and Martial Artist, Bruce Lee who once said, "Don't fear failure. Not failure, but low aim, is the crime. In great attempts it is glorious even to fail."

Resolve today to face your fears and prevent them from stealing your joy from achieving greatness in life.

---

4. Set goals which you are guaranteed to achieve: Success breeds more success

Nothing breeds success like success. In a recent study conducted with online participants researchers found that individuals who experienced success at the start of the experiment went on to producing more success later on.[81]

Associate Professor Arnout van de Rijt said "In each scenario, we found that early success led to more successes... Larger rewards bestowed by our experimentation did not proportionally increase the level of later success. This suggests that a modest initial success may be sufficient to trigger a self-propelling cascade of success in various success-breeds-success scenarios."

The lesson here is that small wins at the start lead to successive wins with more success breeding even more success. So do not despise the small wins, embrace them as they will invariably produce bigger and more glorious victories. Work towards achieving something small, something easy to achieve, a first step, a small task, an initial win.

Though small, it will build into larger and more significant wins. In the end you will look back in amazement at how far you have come, you will be astonished when you see how much ground you have traversed, the barriers you have climbed and the obstacles you have scaled. Don't despise small beginnings.

Sociologist Robert Merton (1968) first coined the term 'The Matthew Effect'[56] after a biblical verse that says "For whoever has will be given more, and they will have an abundance. Whoever does not have, even what they have will be taken from them"(Matthew 25:29; NIV).

This effect occurs in the real world in all areas, including science, sports, and business. It pervades every area of society. On the positive end the effect shows how small, random initial advantages can turn into bigger returns. Winning a regional competition, for example, can lead to winning a national championship, which further leads to becoming the world champion.

John Coates author of the book, *The hour between dog and wolf: Risk-taking, gut feelings and the biology of boom and bust,*[20] cites a study, where researchers meticulously examined data from 630,000 professional tennis matches and discovered that the winner of the first set had a 60% chance of winning the second set, and consequently the match, since a match is based on 3 sets. For these tennis players, initial success lead to further success.

The take home message is to start with small goals which are achievable and realistic and accomplish them first, then climb the ladder, one step at a time, gaining one victory after another.

There is also a negative side of the Matthew effect, lack of success or inequality breeds more failure and inequality. The haves get more, while the have not's get even less.

To overcome your procrastination, plan for small victories at first, and let the benefits you enjoy from these small wins translate into bigger wins and greater victories. Start small but end gloriously big.

Resolve today to think big, but also to think small. First focus all your efforts on achieving the small goals right in front of you, which will allow you to eventually attain your most audacious and magnificent victories.

---

5. Don't underestimate how long a future task will take

There is a psychological phenomenon known as the planning fallacy, where people routinely underestimate how long it will take them to do a future task. Instead of planning 15 minutes to take out the trash, they plan 5 minutes, even though they know there might be inevitable delays along the way.

For example, in my house I regularly clear out the rubbish. It's a quick job which usually takes about 5 minutes to complete. An unplanned situation can arise when someone is in the bathroom when I do the rounds. This is not necessarily a problem, unless I have left the rubbish run to the last 5 minutes before I have to leave for work, or take the kids to school. Not good planning on my part, but an example of how the planning fallacy effects our everyday activities.

The term planning fallacy was first coined by Kahneman and Tversky who described it as tendency people have to "underestimate the time required to complete a project, even when they have considerable experience of past failures to live up to planned schedules."[79]

There is plenty of anecdotal evidence of the planning fallacy. Major construction projects are good examples where planners propose optimistic deadlines which fall far short of predictions. For example, the construction of the International Airport in Denver was opened 16 months late and cost an additional 3.1 billion to complete. When interest payments were added the total cost was 300% above that which was originally predicted. The Sydney Opera House is another good example. The Opera House was planned to be completed in 1963 for $7 million, however only a scaled down version was eventually completed in 1973, ten years later, at a cost of $102 million. In both these examples the initial estimates of time and cost were extremely optimistic, with the end costs for the projects being astronomically out of proportion to the original estimates.

Experimental studies have found the same effect. In one study, Psychology students were asked to estimate how long it would take them to finish their senior thesis. On average they said 33.9 days. The end result was that it took them typically 55.5 days to hand in the completed work, with only 30% handing in their thesis in the time they predicted. In a random survey of Canadian tax payers, it was found that those questioned believed they would mail in their tax returns about a week earlier than they usually would but mailed them in a week later than predicted.[11]

An interesting finding from these studies is that the bias disappears when someone else is doing the forecasting for us. Observers are more pessimistic about the time it will take to complete a task and produce more accurate estimations.

Researchers suggest that compared to you and I, an observer will take into account relevant previous experiences when predicting how long it will take to do a task. They also mention previous obstacles and barriers which in the past slowed progress. You and I are less likely to notice this information, due to our optimistic bias. The take home message is that when you make your next prediction of how long it will take to complete a task, consult someone who can see past your biases and who will make a more realistic prediction of your time frame.

Resolve today to gain a more unbiased assessment of the time required to accomplish a goal. Allow others to feed their untethered views into the equation so that you are more realistic about your goal time frame. This approach is less likely to lead to disappointment.

---

6. Use the power of exercise

One of the big justifications people usually use to keep putting things off is that they feel tired, or they don't have energy. Robin Sharma, author of *The Monk who sold his Ferrari*,[73] believes that one way to beat procrastination is to practice the "second wind workout".

The secret behind the second wind work out is to utilise the natural benefits gained from exercise. Research on the benefits of exercise shows that our bodies release endorphins, dopamine and serotonin, which are chemicals which make us feel good, optimistic and happy. Exercise also increases our metabolism which makes us feel more energised, alert and focused.

By exercising twice per day, once in the morning and once in the early evening, you can boost your energy levels, feel more positive and get more done. Exercise may be the best productivity secret of all.

Sharma may be a bit optimistic here with his second workout idea, because, by my estimations, most people don't even have a 'First Wind Workout'. My advice is to start working out if you are not already doing so. If you are, then consider a second workout as a way of increasing your focus and energy levels to maintain a higher level of productivity throughout your day.

Resolve today to attend to your body's physical needs and enjoy the benefits associated with a healthier fitter lifestyle.

---

7. Create distraction free environments

It is easy to put off doing things when your environment is in a mess, when things are disorganised, or when you can't find what you are looking for to get started in the first place.

Disorder creates distraction. In *Open,*[2] the autobiography of world champion tennis star Andre Agassi, we learn a valuable lesson about organisation and order. This is what Agassi says about how he places supreme order in packing and managing his bag, "No one but me ... can pack the [water] bottles into my bag, along with my clothes and towels and books and shades and wristbands. (My rackets, as always, go in later.) No one but me touches my tennis bag, and when it's finally packed, it stands by the door, like an assassin's kit, a sign that the day has lurched that much closer to the witching hour ... I obsess about my bag. I keep it meticulously organized, and I make no apologies for this anal retentiveness. The bag is my briefcase, suitcase, toolbox, lunchbox, and palette. I need it just right, always. The bag is what I carry onto the court, and what I carry off, two moments when all my senses are extra acute, so I can feel every ounce of its weight. If someone were to slip a pair of argyle socks into my tennis bag, I'd feel it. The tennis bag is a lot like your heart – you have to know what's in it all times."

When you think about it, Agassi's bag is like his office, bedroom or garage. It is that personal space where he gets things done. Like Agassi, when your environment is out of order it can produce a huge psychological barrier to get started. For Agassi no one touches his tennis bag, because when there is disorder in his bag there is disorder in his mind. The point is, to get stuff done requires an organised and ordered environment which invites activity rather than stifles it.

What one thing can you do today to get your environment more organised and ready for you to do your best work pursuing your goals?

---

8. Find an accountability partner

I think one of the most powerful strategies to overcoming procrastination is to find someone to be accountable to. An accountability partner will very likely provide the necessary impetus to get you going, particularly if you feel stalled.

For instance, if your goal is to run 10km's three times per week, find a running buddy to go with you. When you begin running with someone else, it is harder to bail out because you will be disappointing someone else. Just imagine them waiting down the road for you, with their running shoes on, ready to go, while you are at home on the couch missing your appointment with them and the road. According to a study published in Forbes on why 92% of people do not achieve their New Year's resolutions, the primary reason is not having an accountability partner.[33]

When you go looking for an accountability partner, you should find someone who is looking to achieve something similar to what you are aiming for. Find someone who might be at a similar stage to you. For instance, if you just starting to weight train, find someone who is doing the same, otherwise you will be continuously changing weight plates. Furthermore, you should find a communications method that works for you, be that email, texting, or calling by phone.

Which one person could you contact today about becoming your accountability partner?

---

9. Fake it till you make it

You may have heard the term 'fake it till you make it', which means that by faking a behaviour, skill, or emotion, you will eventually develop the behaviour or skill, or experience the emotion.

For example, if you stand in front of a mirror and smile while looking at your reflection, you will begin to feel happier. Studies show that fake smiling will improve your mood and lower your stress. For instance, one study showed that people experienced more physiological and psychological benefits when asked to smile while doing stressful tasks, compared to the people who were not asked to smile while doing the same task.[51]

Another 'fake it till you make it' experiment has shown that if you hold your body in a 'high-power' pose for short periods of time, you can literally summon a surge of power and well-being needed for the moment.

Examples of power stances include the classic feet on desk, hands behind head and standing and leaning on one's hands over a desk. These power stances stimulate the release of testosterone (the hormone responsible for power and dominance) and lower levels of cortisol (a stress hormone which can impact and impair your immunity, cause hypertension and precipitate memory loss).

The research on power stances shows that striking power poses can increase your feelings of power and increase your tolerance to risk.[16] If you are wondering what low power positions are, and which you should avoid if you are trying to ramp up your mojo, then don't sit in a chair with your arms held close to your body, or fold your hands or sit with your arms and legs crossed tightly. These positions are not likely to ramp up your testosterone, or make you feel more confident.

Resolve today not to wait until you feel the desired emotion, rather behave in a way which suggests you are already experiencing it.

---

10. Throw out your demand for perfection

Perfectionism can often become an excuse for procrastination and you can see why. The need to attain flawless, excessively high standards, which are usually accompanied by unreasonable self-criticism and negative self-evaluations, is hard to ignore. Add to this the worry of what others think about you, and you have a recipe for never getting anything started.

Rather than go through all the turmoil of attaining perfection or receiving criticism, the easier path is to not do the task at all. The origins of perfectionism may go back to your childhood when you were punished for your mistakes. In the old days teachers would routinely hit kids over their knuckles for not writing their letters correctly or making simple math mistakes. This was a good recipe to indoctrinate children (namely you and me) with the need for perfectionism. After all, imperfection meant pain, while perfection meant praise or at least an absence of pain, and if you were lucky a positive affirmation from teachers (good boy for writing your letters so neatly).

Of course, perfectionism has its place. For example, there are many professions where you would be quite happy for a practitioner to be a perfectionist. Most people would prefer their plastic surgeon or heart surgeon to do a perfect job on their face or heart. Wouldn't you want the best outcome for your new nose job or heart transplant? On the surface, this sounds good, but look a little deeper and you will notice the dark side of perfectionism even for professions like this.

For instance, your heart surgeon might take so long with your transplant, trying to get every step perfect that you eventually die on the operating table. Now perfectionism isn't so great is it? Perfectionism brings with it the tendency to take too long to complete a task which can have serious ramifications.

Many people are reluctant to get started in the first place, because they can't stand the idea of having to spend so long doing something.

One way to mitigate the effects of perfectionism is to set a "good is enough" standard which once reached is the point at which the task is deemed complete. This can be useful in any situation. It also makes use of the 80/20 principle which says that 80% of your outputs are achieved with just 20% of your inputs.

Most tasks are practically complete after the most important 20% of the work is done. The rest is just fluff.

Resolve today to find a 'good enough standard', after which you move on to the next task.

---

11. Accept that your job is never finished

Your job is never finished, so learning to live with this fact will free you up to live a richer and more rewarding life. It will also help you get started on certain tasks over which you have been procrastinating.

Previous experience may have blemished certain tasks, which proved too draining in the past. For one reason or another, back then you willingly gave your time to complete jobs which left you scared. Now being a bit wiser, you are reluctant to do it all over again.

Instead of throwing the proverbial baby out with the bathwater, maybe you should be clearer about your boundaries. For example, Richard Branson finds plenty of time to spend on his private island, even though he is very busy managing 400 companies.

Facebook COO Sheryl Sandberg likewise finds plenty of time with her family and leaves work at 5pm every day to go home and have dinner with her kids. President Bush had time to read 95 books per year, and Andy Grove former Intel president would arrive at 8am and leave at 6pm consistently. Grove, wrote a book *High Output Management*[37] in which he reveals his secret.

Part of his success is that he goes home when he is tired, rather than when the work is done. The truth is that the work is never all done, and there is always going to be more and more work to do.

Starting today, give yourself permission to accept that the job will never be over. The secret is not to allow this to prevent you starting today on your goals, and achieving the life you want.

---

12. Use the 'fear of loss' as a motivator

Many studies show that people are far more motivated by loss than gain.[79] Most studies suggest that the psychological effect of loss is twice as powerful as gain. You are more motivated to keep the $100 you already have than to gain an extra $100.

It reminds me of an English phrase, "A bird in the hand is worth two in the bush" which suggests that we are happier with the one bird we already have than the prospect of gaining two more. A sure thing is more valuable than an uncertain gamble. So why not put this loss aversion tactic to work and use it to help you break through procrastination.

One way you can do this is to deliberately put yourself in the path of loss. Remember you are more afraid of loss than gain. If you really want to kick the annoying tendency to procrastinate on a particular goal, sign up to www.stickk.com, (a Yale University initiative). On this site you can establish a binding agreement with yourself in the form of a signed contract, to acknowledge the commitment it will take to accomplish your goal.

To leverage this commitment, you will put money on the line; an amount you can choose yourself. Then find a referee to verify your progress and find supporters to cheer you on your path to success. According to the site, a referee doubles your chances of success.

Placing a financial stake on your goal triples your chances of succeeding. You can choose who will receive the stake should you fail to achieve your goal, be it your favourite charity or your mother in law.

If you are averse to the idea of using an online provider to hold your stake, you can use your friends or family members. You can place $100 for example in a kitty and agree to donate it to a charity if you do not achieve your goal by the said date. Give the kitty to someone you trust to hold, and if you do not fulfil your agreement, they are to donate the money on your behalf.

This method of loss aversion works particularly well on goals you have been procrastinating on for some time, for example; if you had a goal of losing 10kg, quitting smoking, or starting an exercise program. In these cases, you can start by leveraging small amounts of money like $10 to get the process rolling.

The inevitable conclusion is that you will probably default on your agreement as you have before because the stakes are low, but in this case you will experience loss, though small, but still effective. For one you will have to face the fact that you have failed to achieve your goal, and you will have to face another person who is holding the money and admit failure.

Don't stop here, the next move is to increase the monetary stake significantly, to say $100 or $250. Your chances of success will be tripled as the stakes have now increased exponentially, and you will be more inclined to prove to yourself and others that this time you will succeed, plus you have a lot more money to lose.

Resolve today to make a firm commitment to get started on your most important goals and if you find yourself procrastinating, use your fear of loss to motivate you.

---

13. Do what self-made millionaires do

Thomas Corley, author of "Change Your Habits, Change Your Life", spent 5 years studying the habits of self-made millionaires. A self-made millionaire is someone who has worked for his or her success; someone who did not gain wealth through gambling, lotto or any other arbitrary means. They also did not inherit it!

Corley discovered one habit which keeps millions of people from becoming rich, but which is avoided by people who eventually strike it rich. According to Corley the one thing you won't hear self-made millionaires saying is, "I'll do it tomorrow!"

Corley says that procrastination is a habit avoided by self-made millionaires. He discovered this after studying the daily habits of 177 self- made millionaires over the course of 5 years. Self-made millionaires got that way by developing the habit of *doing it now*. They don't put things off till tomorrow, or wait till the last minute to do them.

Self-made millionaires also have a passion for what they do. They love their work, which is a far cry from how millions of other people view their work.

Corley says that only 13% of employees are really engaged or emotionally invested in their work. The rest, are disinterested, un-invested, struggle financially and lose credibility with their employers and colleagues. This consequently spills over negatively into other key areas of their business performance. The consequence is that everyone suffers. Corley says that we like to do the things we like to do, and avoid the things we don't like. If you don't have a passion for what you are doing, then tasks related to your job will be relegated to the end of the list.

A few ways self-made millionaires use to overcome procrastination include:

- Following action or to-do lists

- Creating strict deadlines

- Meeting with accountability partners, or someone who will hold them responsible for keeping goals and deadlines

---

Resolve today to follow the example of self-made millionaires and stop procrastinating.

Exercise 1

Make a plan to tackle your areas of procrastination. For each area of procrastination you have, identify what is stopping you from progressing it and which techniques presented in this chapter can be applied to help you achieve your goal.

CONCLUSION

Moving Towards Your Best Self

"There is nothing noble in being superior to your fellow man; true nobility is being superior to your former self."

Ernest Hemingway

Congratulations on reaching the end of the book. By doing so you have demonstrated your willingness to learn and invest in your future. I have read that less that 10% of people who buy a new book read past the first chapter.[65] This is a shocking statistic if you ask me, because to a certain degree it demonstrates how much effort people are willing to put in to developing their minds. According to reading statistics published by Statistics Brain in September 2016, 80% of Americans said they did not buy a book in the previous 12 months, while 70% said they had not been in a bookstore in the past 5 years. Furthermore, 42% of college students will never read another book after they graduate.[10] What a pity, as reading is a primary means to developing your mind.

As a way of summarising the many principles and ideas discussed in the previous chapters, I would like to retell a touching story I read in George Tan's book *Success Secrets*. Tan relates an account when psychologist Bill O'Hanlon, while appearing on the Oprah Winfrey Show in 1999, was asked by a woman if he could recommend 3 psychotherapists like him whom she could contact for help. She had been struggling for years with a debilitating drug addiction, which she just couldn't shake and desperately needed help to change.

O'Hanlon recommended 3 psychotherapists he believed could help her, and that was the last time he heard from her, until one year later. During that time, she had contacted all three psychotherapists, but she couldn't afford their fees, so she decided to heal herself.

At that time, she was taking 27 pills per day. She was so badly addicted, that reducing her daily intake by even 1 pill was all but impossible. It was an awful situation. However, she was motivated to get better and came up with a surprisingly clever plan which only someone with her level of determination would contemplate. She decided that she would scrape off a tiny bit from each pill every day.

Her actions were small but measurable. They were minute, but meaningful. Each day, little by little, she would scrape more and more off her pills, until finally there was nothing left to scrape off. She had done it. She had broken her addiction. She was victorious. She had won the battle. After 10 months, she emerged the victor, having achieved her goal. At that moment you can say she had achieved her best self.

Her story retells many of the principles and ideas relayed in this book. She had a No 1 Goal; to shake a debilitating drug addiction. The accomplishment of this one goal impacted her entire life. Once achieved, she was able to solve many of the other problems she was experiencing in her life.

Her story also illustrates the amazing power of achieving small incremental goals. At that time, the jump from her current predicament to her desired state was too big to take in one leap. She needed many steps. Had she underestimated the impact of each small step, she would have never realised her goal. This reminds me of what Peter Drucker once said, "We greatly overestimate what we can accomplish in one year, but we greatly underestimate what we can accomplish in five years." Your gradual advancements might not look like much now, but 5 years from now, when you look back you will be aghast at how much you have achieved.

Her story illustrates the power of grit and self-discipline; 2 of the cornerstones of great achievement. She had to show great self-discipline in the daily action of shaving off small bits from her pills. At first it would have been difficult, the first few days the hardest. Her determination to succeed and her self-discipline to shave small bits off each pill, would have turned into a daily habit. Once established, the process would have become easier. She would have grown in self-confidence and her self- esteem would have blossomed.

Dr William James believed, "the greatest revolution of my generation is the discovery that individuals, by changing their inner attitude of mind, can change the outer aspects of their lives."

This has been one of the central messages of this book. The inner aspects of your subconscious mind can be nurtured to create the life you want. By continually sowing daily the seed of change into your mind, will ensure that the seed will take root and begin to grow.

At first the growth will be slow, the changes will be small. At times so small they will be barely recognisable. The little seed slowly spreads its roots into your mind. It slowly changes your beliefs, your attitudes, your thoughts. Before long you notice your outer reality beginning to change. The things you scarcely believed were possible begin to emerge. You start noticing your goals, dreams and ambitions materialising in the world around you. This is what it means to achieve your best self. Your best self is realised when you align your beliefs, thoughts and feelings with your outer world. The two emerge and become one.

There is an important mental law which suggests that whatever is impressed is expressed. Whatever you deeply impress into your subconscious mind will express itself in your outer world.

When you sow the seed of what you want daily into your mind; when you water that seed and allow it to grow, it takes on a power of its own. Positive thinking is not enough. You must have positive knowing if you hope to achieve your best dreams. You need to be completely convinced that you are able to achieve your goals. At first you may not be, but as time passes, and as you work daily sowing the seed and taking small measurable action, your faith will grow and your belief will be strengthened.

WHAT DOES IT TAKE TO ACHIEVE YOUR BEST SELF

To conclude, lets briefly revisit some of the key points and ideas covered in this book.

1. Develop clarity for what you want

The first step to achieving your best self is to have clarity about what you want. To discover what you want, you can engage in no limits thinking. Consider what your life might be like 5 years from now, if you had absolutely no limits imposed on you. Charles Garfield called it "Blue Sky Thinking." Imagine that all things are possible for you, and you are looking into a clear blue sky with no limits. William Marsden said, "realize what you really want. It stops you from chasing butterflies and puts you to work digging gold." Gaining clarity is essential to great achievement, but it is also one of the most difficult aspects to accomplish.

2. Set goals to achieve what you want

Once you have clarity about what you want , you should set SMART goals for each item on your list. SMART goals help you to think through the key elements of your goals and ensure your goals are specific, measurable, actionable, achievable, realistic, relevant, and have a realistic time frame. Once you have honestly worked through each element, and ensured that your goals align with your values, you will have an excellent chance of achieving them. If you do not test your goals against your core values, you might run the risk of spending your life pursuing the wrong objectives. You might reach the top of the ladder only to discover you were climbing up the wrong wall.

3. Imprint your goals onto your subconscious mind

To achieve your goals, continuously sow their seed into your subconscious mind and constantly water that seed to help it grow. Never stop sowing the seeds of change into your mind. After a short time, your goals will begin to saturate your thinking. You will automate the subconscious process of goal pursuit and attainment. Your actions will continuously be directed in the direction of your most important goals. You will discover that you begin to draw the things you want into your life. Your dreams become reality, because whatever you think about most of the time finds a path to your door. Use the goal achievers journal or similar method to expose your mind to your goals on a daily basis.

4. Use self-discipline to develop new habits and routines

Learn from successful people in your field, and discover what habits they have developed which helped them succeed. Emulate their habits and adapt them into your own life. Be self-disciplined and change your behaviour. Develop habits like getting up earlier, writing out your goals daily, respecting your time and that of others, taking care of your spiritual health, looking after your body and continually learning and developing your mind.

5. Take action on your goals

One of the primary differences between high and low achievers is their level of 'action orientation'. High achievers are always in pursuit of their most important goals, while low achievers are always in pursuit of their next excuse. Low achievers are usually full of good intentions. There is a saying that the road to Hell is paved with good intentions.

6. Never stop trying

Successful people fail far more than unsuccessful people do, because they never stop trying. Successful people have developed high levels of grit, one of the key attributes supported by science which correlates with achievement of long term goals. High achievers keep going even though they lose, get knocked down and are unsuccessful more times than they care to remember. When the going gets tough, low achievers bail out and throw in the towel, but high achievers press on, bit by bit until they reach the summit.

7. Face your fears

Fear is most likely the biggest factor in keeping people trapped in mediocrity. People are afraid of losing the status quo, which provides them with just enough comfort to get by. This comes at a cost, as they are destined to live unfulfilled lives filled with regret and disappointment. Many people seem to build their house on a foundation of fear, but people who show courage get remembered. They make their mark on the world and play an important role in affecting people's lives. People who are willing to face their fears generally step out with courage and take more risks.

8. Don't procrastinate.

Non-procrastinators get started today on their most important goals, not tomorrow or next week. If you keep putting off till tomorrow what you should be doing today then your goals will go nowhere. Procrastination is expensive; it costs you in time, money and energy. Overcoming procrastination is to your benefit. You do today what others plan to do tomorrow. In doing so you make progress on your dreams and ambitions, while others watch theirs slip into oblivion. Achieving your best self can only be achieved by getting busy today on your highest dreams and goals. So what are you waiting for, the journey starts now.

About the Author

Dr David Barton has a desire to see more people achieving more of their potential in life. He believes that people have almost infinite potential, which if they learned to access, would transform their lives beyond their wildest dreams.

Dr Barton has a PhD in Psychology from Otago University, New Zealand. He has worked in clinical practice helping others find better strategies for achieving their goals.

Dr Barton enjoys speaking, teaching and writing. He is an avid reader and student of psychology, motivation, business, self-help, health, and religion.

In the past Dr Barton has worked in a variety of fields such as Telecommunications, IT, Sales, and has run his own businesses.

Currently he lives in Dunedin, New Zealand with his wife, three daughters and other family members who live nearby.

If you would like Dr Barton to speak to your organisation please feel free to contact him directly:

David Barton Training
PO Box 8009
Gardens, Dunedin, 9041
Otago, New Zealand
www.davidbartontraining.com
Email: davidbarton@davidbartontraining.com

References

1   AFL-CIO, '100 Highest Paid Ceos'2014)
        <http://www.aflcio.org/Corporate-Watch/Paywatch-
        2014/100-Highest-Paid-CEOs>2016].
2   Andre Agassi, *Open* (Plon, 2011).
3   R Alexander, 'Annual Earning'2012)
        <http://www.bbc.com/news/magazine-17312819> [Accessed
        2016 2016].
4   David Allen, *Getting Things Done: The Art of Stress-Free
        Productivity* (Hachette UK, 2015).
5   Scientific American, 'Computers Versus Brains'2011)
        <http://www.scientificamerican.com/article/computers-vs-
        brains/>.
6   Vladimir M Berginer, 'Neurological Aspects of the David-
        Goliath Battle: Restriction in the Giant's Visual Field', *The Israel
        Medical Association journal: IMAJ*, 2 (2000), 725-27.
7   Ellen Berscheid, and Elaine Hatfield, 'Interpersonal Attraction',
        (1969).
8   The Conference Board., 'Job Satisfaction: 2014 Edition'2014)
        <https://www.conference-
        board.org/publications/publicationdetail.cfm?publicationid=2
        785>2016].
9   Statistics Brain, 'New Years Resolution Statistics'2015)
        <http://www.statisticbrain.com/new-years-resolution-
        statistics/> [Accessed January 2016].
10   Statistics Brain., 'Reading Statistics'2016)
        <http://www.statisticbrain.com/reading-statistics/>2016].
11   Roger Buehler, Dale Griffin, and Michael Ross, 'Exploring the"
        Planning Fallacy": Why People Underestimate Their Task
        Completion Times', *Journal of personality and social psychology*, 67
        (1994), 366.
12   Jane B Burka, and Lenora M Yuen, *Procrastination: Why You Do
        It, What to Do About It Now* (Da Capo Press, 2008).
13   Tony Buzan, *Mind Mapping* (Pearson Education, 2006).
14   Donn Erwin Byrne, *The Attraction Paradigm*. Vol. 11 (Academic
        Pr, 1971).
15   Jack Canfield, '"How Am I Doing?" the One Question That Can
        Change All of Your Relationships'2009)

<http://www.huffingtonpost.com/jack-canfield/how-am-i-doing-the-one-qu_b_268600.html>.

16 Dana R Carney, Amy JC Cuddy, and Andy J Yap, 'Power Posing Brief Nonverbal Displays Affect Neuroendocrine Levels and Risk Tolerance', *Psychological Science,* 21 (2010), 1363-68.

17 Lewis Carroll, 'Alice's Adventures in Wonderland the Complete Illustrated Works of Lewis Carroll', (London: Chancellor Press, 1865).

18 Luigi Cattaneo, and Giacomo Rizzolatti, 'The Mirror Neuron System', *Archives of neurology,* 66 (2009), 557-60.

19 Nicholas A Christakis, and James H Fowler, *Connected: The Surprising Power of Our Social Networks and How They Shape Our Lives* (Little, Brown, 2009).

20 John Coates, *The Hour between Dog and Wolf: Risk-Taking, Gut Feelings and the Biology of Boom and Bust* (HarperCollins UK, 2012).

21 Richard A Dienstbier, 'Arousal and Physiological Toughness: Implications for Mental and Physical Health', *Psychological review,* 96 (1989), 84.

22 Robert E Dohrenwend, 'The Sling: Forgotten Firepower of Antiquity', *Journal of Martial Arts,* 11 (2002), 28-49.

23 George T Doran, 'There'sa Smart Way to Write Management's Goals and Objectives', *Management review,* 70 (1981), 35-36.

24 Windy Dryden, *Overcoming Procrastination* (Sheldon, 2000).

25 Angela Duckworth, 'Grit: The Power of Passion and Perseverance', Ted Talks, (2013) <https://www.ted.com/talks/angela_lee_duckworth_grit_the_power_of_passion_and_perseverance/transcript?language=en> [Accessed 2015.

26 Angela L Duckworth, Christopher Peterson, Michael D Matthews, and Dennis R Kelly, 'Grit: Perseverance and Passion for Long-Term Goals', *Journal of personality and social psychology,* 92 (2007), 1087.

27 Charles Duhigg, *The Power of Habit: Why We Do What We Do in Life and Business.* Vol. 34 (Random House, 2012).

28 Wayne D Dyer, *Your Erroneous Zones* (Avon, 1976).

29 Robert A Emmons, and Michael E McCullough, 'Counting Blessings Versus Burdens: An Experimental Investigation of

Gratitude and Subjective Well-Being in Daily Life', *Journal of personality and social psychology*, 84 (2003), 377.

30   K Anders Ericsson, *The Road to Excellence: The Acquisition of Expert Performance in the Arts and Sciences, Sports, and Games* (Psychology Press, 2014).

31   Reza Falahati, 'The Relationship between Students' Iq and Their Ability to Use Transitional Words and Expressions in Writing', *Working Papers of the Linguistics Circle,* 17 (2010), 11-19.

32   Michael Lawrence Faulkner, and Michelle Faulkner-Lunsford, *Top 100 Power Verbs: The Most Powerful Verbs and Phrases You Can Use to Win in Any Situation* (FT Press, 2013).

33   Forbes, 'Just 8% of People Achieve Their New Year's Resolutions. Here's How They Do It'2016)March 2016].

34   R. Frank, 'Millionaires Living in the USA'2016) <http://www.cnbc.com/2016/03/07/record-number-of-millionaires-living-in-the-us.html>2016].

35   Malcolm Gladwell, *David and Goliath: Underdogs, Misfits and the Art of Battling Giants* (Penguin UK, 2013).

36   Malcolm. Gladwell, *Outliers: The Story of Success* (Hachette UK, 2008).

37   Andrew S Grove, *High Output Management* (Vintage Books New York, NY, 1985).

38   Jon Hamilton, 'Think You're Multitasking? Think Again', *Morning Edition, National Public Radio (2 October 2008)* (2008).

39   Darren Hardy, *The Compound Effect* (Vanguard, 2011).

40   Nathan Hewitt, '10 Benefits of Fasting That Will Surprise You'2015) <http://www.lifehack.org/articles/lifestyle/10-benefits-of-fasting-that-will-surprise-you.html>2015].

41   Napoleon Hill, *Napoleon Hill's Unlimited Success: 52 Steps to Personal & Financial Reward* (Piatkus, 1994).

42   Napoleon. Hill, 'Think and Grow Rich. Greenwich, Connecticut', (Fawcett Publications, Inc, 1961).

43   E Hirsch, JH Cuadros, and JE Backofen, 'David's Choice: A Sling and Tactical Advantage', in *Jerusalem, Israel: 15th International Symposium on Ballistics* (1995), pp. 11-20.

44   Marco Iacoboni, Istvan Molnar-Szakacs, Vittorio Gallese, Giovanni Buccino, John C Mazziotta, and Giacomo Rizzolatti, 'Grasping the Intentions of Others with One's Own Mirror Neuron System', *PLoS Biol,* 3 (2005), e79.

45   Sheena S Iyengar, and Mark R Lepper, 'When Choice Is Demotivating: Can One Desire Too Much of a Good Thing?', *Journal of personality and social psychology*, 79 (2000), 995.

46   Michael Jordan, 'Thoughts of the Business of Life', Forbes Quotes, (<http://www.forbes.com/quotes/11194/>2016].

47   John Kehoe, *Money, Success and You* (Zoetic, 1990).

48   Gary Keller, and Jay Papasan, 'The One Thing: The Surprisingly Truth Behind Extraordinary Results', (Abril, 2013).

49   Kruse Kevin., *15 Secrets Successful People Know About Time Management: The Productivity Habits of 7 Billionaires, 13 Olympic Athletes, 29 Straight-a Students, and 239 Entrepreneurs* (USA: The Kruse Group; 1 edition, 2015), p. 202.

50   Richard Koch, *The 80/20 Principle: The Secret to Achieving More with Less* (Crown Business, 2011).

51   Tara L Kraft, and Sarah D Pressman, 'Grin and Bear It the Influence of Manipulated Facial Expression on the Stress Response', *Psychological science*, 23 (2012), 1372-78.

52   Ellen J Langer, Arthur Blank, and Benzion Chanowitz, 'The Mindlessness of Ostensibly Thoughtful Action: The Role of" Placebic" Information in Interpersonal Interaction', *Journal of personality and social psychology*, 36 (1978), 635.

53   Sing Lau, 'The Effect of Smiling on Person Perception', *The Journal of Social Psychology*, 117 (1982), 63-67.

54   Robert L Leahy, *The Worry Cure: Seven Steps to Stop Worry from Stopping You* (Harmony Books, 2006).

55   Edwin A. Locke, and Gary P. Latham, 'New Directions in Goal-Setting Theory', *Current Directions in Psychological Science*, 15 (2006), 265-68.

56   Robert K Merton, 'The Matthew Effect in Science', *Science*, 159 (1968), 56-63.

57   George A Miller, 'The Magical Number Seven, Plus or Minus Two: Some Limits on Our Capacity for Processing Information', *Psychological review*, 63 (1956), 81.

58   Walter Mischel, Ebbe B Ebbesen, and Antonette Raskoff Zeiss, 'Cognitive and Attentional Mechanisms in Delay of Gratification', *Journal of personality and social psychology*, 21 (1972), 204.

59   Pam A Mueller, and Daniel M Oppenheimer, 'The Pen Is Mightier Than the Keyboard Advantages of Longhand over

Laptop Note Taking', *Psychological science* (2014), 0956797614524581.

60   Gene O'Kelly, *Chasing Daylight: How My Forthcoming Death Transformed My Life* (McGraw Hill Professional, 2007).

61   Jeff Olson, *The Slight Edge: Secret to a Successful Life* (Video Plus, 2005).

62   James W Pennebaker, 'Putting Stress into Words: Health, Linguistic, and Therapeutic Implications', *Behaviour research and therapy,* 31 (1993), 539-48.

63   Oscar Raymundo, 'Richard Branson: The Advice Entrepreneurs Thank Me for the Most', Inc. Magazene, (2014) <http://www.inc.com/oscar-raymundo/richard-branson-advice-entrepreneurs-thank-me-for-the-most.html>2015].

64   Roy Morgan Research., 'Digital Vs Traditional Media in New Zealand'2013) <http://www.roymorgan.com/findings/5201-digital-traditional-media-new-zealand-201309200004> [Accessed 26/09/2016 2016].

65   Tony Robbins, *Awaken the Giant Within: How to Take Immediate Control of Your Mental, Emotional, Physical and Financial* (Simon and Schuster, 2007).

66   Lindsay A Robertson, Helena M McAnally, and Robert J Hancox, 'Childhood and Adolescent Television Viewing and Antisocial Behavior in Early Adulthood', *Pediatrics,* 131 (2013), 439-46.

67   Jim Rohn, 'Cultivating Your Enterprising Nature' <http://www.nightingale.com/articles/cultivating-your-enterprising-nature/> [Accessed 13/10/2016 2016].

68   Robert Rosenthal, and Lenore F Jacobson, 'Teacher Expectations for the Disadvantaged', *Scientific American,* 218 (1968), 19-23.

69   Michael H Rosove, 'Race to the End: Amundsen, Scott and the Attainment of the South Pole. Rde Mcphee. 2010. New York, London: Sterling Innovation (American Museum of Natural History, in Association with the Scott Polar Research Institute, University of Cambridge). X+ 245p., Illustrated, Hard Cover. Isbn 978-1-4027-7029-6. Us $27.95, C $35.95', *Polar Record,* 47 (2011), 275-77.

70   Alice Schroeder, *The Snowball: Warren Buffett and the Business of Life* (A&C Black, 2009).

71   Social Security, 'National Average Wage Index'2014)
        <https://www.ssa.gov/oact/cola/AWI.html> [Accessed 2016
        2016].
72   Peter Sedlmeier, Juliane Eberth, Marcus Schwarz, Doreen
        Zimmermann, Frederik Haarig, Sonia Jaeger, and Sonja Kunze,
        'The Psychological Effects of Meditation: A Meta-Analysis',
        Psychological bulletin, 138 (2012), 1139.
73   Robin S Sharma, *The Monk Who Sold His Ferrari* (Element, 2004).
74   Barbara Sher, *I Could Do Anything If I Only Knew What It Was:
        How to Discover What You Really Want and How to Get It* (Dell,
        2010).
75   Richard St John, *The 8 Traits Successful People Have in Common*
        (Embassy Books, 2011).
76   U.S. Bureau of Labor Statistics., 'Charts from the American
        Time Use Survey'2014)
        <http://www.bls.gov/tus/charts/home.htm#about>.
77   Dianne M Tice, and Roy F Baumeister, 'Longitudinal Study of
        Procrastination, Performance, Stress, and Health: The Costs and
        Benefits of Dawdling', *Psychological science* (1997), 454-58.
78   Brian Tracy, *Eat That Frog!: 21 Great Ways to Stop Procrastinating
        and Get More Done in Less Time* (Berrett-Koehler Publishers,
        2007).
79   Amos Tversky, and Daniel Kahneman, 'Loss Aversion in
        Riskless Choice: A Reference-Dependent Model', *The quarterly
        journal of economics* (1991), 1039-61.
80   Hal Urban, *Life's Greatest Lessons: 20 Things That Matter* (Simon
        and Schuster, 2005).
81   Arnout van de Rijt, Soong Moon Kang, Michael Restivo, and
        Akshay Patil, 'Field Experiments of Success-Breeds-Success
        Dynamics', *Proceedings of the National Academy of Sciences,* 111
        (2014), 6934-39.
82   Denis Waitley, *Psychology of Winning* (Berkley, 1985).
83   Bronnie Ware, *The Top Five Regrets of the Dying: A Life
        Transformed by the Dearly Departing* (Hay House, Inc, 2012).
84   Drew Westen, Lorelle J Burton, and Robin Kowalski,
        Psychology: Australian and New Zealand Edition (John Wiley &
        Sons Australia, Ltd., 2006).

References

85   Katherine S Wheeler, 'The Relationships between Television Viewing Behaviors, Attachment, Loneliness, Depression, and Psychological Well-Being', (2015).

86   James Emery White, 'You Can Experience the Spiritual Life (Nashville, Tn', (Word Publishing, 1999).

87   H William, and Steven L Gortmaker, 'Do We Fatten Our Children at the Television Set? Obesity and Television Viewing in Children and Adolescents', *Pediatrics (USA)* (1985).

88   Fadel Zeidan, Katherine T Martucci, Robert A Kraft, John G McHaffie, and Robert C Coghill, 'Neural Correlates of Mindfulness Meditation-Related Anxiety Relief', *Social cognitive and affective neuroscience,* 9 (2014), 751-59.

Index

www.ingramcontent.com/pod-product-compliance
Lightning Source LLC
LaVergne TN
LVHW011219080426
835509LV00005B/203